MEN
of the
BIBLE
DEVOTIONAL

MEN
of the
BIBLE
DEVOTIONAL

**Insights from the
WARRIORS, WIMPS,
and WISE GUYS**

BARBOUR BOOKS
An Imprint of Barbour Publishing, Inc.

Print ISBN 978-1-68322-485-3

Published by Barbour Books, an imprint of Barbour Publishing, Inc., P.O. Box 719, Uhrichsville, Ohio 44683, www.barbourbooks.com

Our mission is to inspire the world with the life-changing message of the Bible.

Printed in the United States of America.

Welcome to the MEN of the BIBLE Devotional

The men of the Bible are a colorful group of people. Some, like Abraham, give us a powerful picture of faith. Others, like King Saul or King Ahab, offer us serious warnings against sin. Then there are the seemingly unremarkable men, many of whom get only one passing mention in scripture, whose lives seem much like our own.

Every man in the Bible has a story, however, whether short or long, and through each, God shows us some eternal truth. Sometimes these men help us understand an important spiritual principle, or they illustrate a problem we've faced in our own barely functional or clearly faith-filled lives. But whatever the success level of a biblical man's life—or our own—one truth remains secure: God shines His enduring love through every believer's life.

God loves men—those who lived thousands of years ago and those of us who live today, and His Holy Spirit can sustain and transform us today just as He did those of long ago. By their examples, the men described in these pages lead us through the rough-and-tumble circumstances of this world with the strength and peace that comes from knowing God.

As a bonus to the stories of these biblical men, this volume includes alphabetical lists of the meanings of some men's names that appear in the Bible. These appear on pages 17, 28, 39, 50, 61, 72, 83, 94, 105, 116, 127, 138, 149, 160, 171, 182, and 191.

ADAM: Made in the Image of His Creator

*Then God said, "Let us make mankind in our image,
in our likeness, so that they may rule over the fish
in the sea and the birds in the sky, over the
livestock and all the wild animals, and over all
the creatures that move along the ground."*

Genesis 1:26 NIV

God made Adam—and every human after him—in His own image. That can mean a lot of things, but it doesn't mean Adam was like God in that he possessed all knowledge and power over everything, or that he was like God in that he was perfect in his love and holiness. Adam was a created being, and though he would live eternally, he had a beginning. God, on the other hand, always was and always will be.

First and foremost, "created in God's image" means that the Lord made humans as the only living things on earth with a true consciousness of their Creator. While all created things owe their existence to their Creator, only humans can truly know and love the One who made them.

God had spent the first six days of creation making the cosmos, the earth, and plants and animals. All of those things are in their own ways reflections of God the Creator, but none of them truly bore His image the way the first man did.

That's because God wanted people to see Him in all creation—and because He wanted a loving, personal Creator/created relationship with the only beings He truly created in His own image—us!

MORDECAI: Honorable in Exile

*Mordecai. . .was very great among the Jews,
who held him in high esteem, because he continued
to work for the good of his people and to speak
up for the welfare of all their descendants.*

Esther 10:3 NLT

Mordecai had been carried into exile to Babylon, where he brought up a cousin who had been orphaned. His cousin, known by the Babylonian name of Esther, later become the queen to King Xerxes. Mordecai then discovered a plot to assassinate the king. Despite being in a foreign country and under a foreign king, Mordecai exposed the plot and it was foiled. His loyalty was recorded in the annals of the king, although nothing was done at the time to reward him.

Later, Mordecai refused to bow to Haman, a high government official, who then began plotting against the Jews in general and Mordecai in particular. But during a sleepless night, King Xerxes had the chronicles read to him and realized that Mordecai hadn't been rewarded. Then Queen Esther brought Haman's plot against the Jews to the attention of Xerxes—who became furious. He ordered Haman to be hanged on the gallows built for Mordecai. The king then promoted Mordecai to Haman's vacant position.

Through all of this, Mordecai had acted in an honorable way. He did so without expecting a reward and without asking for one. His concern was for others—the king, Esther, and his fellow Jews. Looking out for others brought great reward to him as well.

POTIPHAR: He Couldn't See the Plan

When Joseph was taken to Egypt by the Ishmaelite traders,
he was purchased by Potiphar, an Egyptian officer.
Potiphar was captain of the guard for
Pharaoh, the king of Egypt.
Genesis 39:1 NLT

Who knows what he wanted when he dropped by the local market? But instead of picking up milk and eggs, Potiphar bought a slave. Not just any slave, but the grandson of Abraham. And not just the grandson of Abraham, but the man God ultimately used to save both Egypt and the Israelites.

Even in Joseph's slavery, God had a plan.

It didn't take long for Potiphar to trust this Israelite with everything he owned. The longer Joseph remained in his house, the better things seemed to go for Potiphar, whose crops and livestock increased. This royal officer must have believed that "luck" played a key role in his purchase of Joseph, but no luck was involved.

The last thing we read about Potiphar is that he tossed Joseph in prison based on a false accusation.

Even in the false accusation, God had a plan.

Potiphar's story was over, but Joseph's was just getting started. Most likely Potiphar was alive to see his former slave become the second in command in the entire country of Egypt.

God always has a plan (Romans 8:28). Sometimes He just wants us to follow where He leads so we can see the story unfold firsthand.

GAIUS: Honorable Mention!

I thank God that I did not baptize
any of you except Crispus and Gaius.
1 Corinthians 1:14 NIV

It's encouraging to be noticed, but we often want more than that.

When some of the Corinthian believers were bragging about who had brought the Gospel to them or who had baptized them, Paul took them to task like a frustrated parent, asking who did the work in them? Did Paul or Cephas, or was it the Messiah?

Gaius, while only mentioned, is one of a few Corinthians Paul baptized, and apparently one that he was confident wasn't going to brag about who dipped him. That was more than being noticed. It was being found quietly trustworthy.

Many believers don't do anything that others would notice, but they are steady and dependable. Some quietly give shelter to visitors, feed travelers, give funds, or pray faithfully.

Gaius showed up later as Paul's host on his third missionary journey. In fact, Gaius was host to the entire local church, which met in his home. He was still trustworthy and had now shown himself hospitable and concerned with the well-being of his fellow believers.

Gaius was given honorable mention because he was honorable in his faith.

JOHN: Fisherman Becomes Fisher of Men

[Jesus] saw two other brothers, James son of Zebedee and his brother John. They were in a boat with their father Zebedee, preparing their nets. Jesus called them, and immediately they left the boat and their father and followed him.

Matthew 4:21–22 NIV

How often do we immediately do what we're told? That's exactly what the Bible says John and his brother James did.

It was probably just another day for John, not much different than any other. He was a fisherman on Lake Galilee, like his father and his brother, and they were in a boat near the shore preparing their nets. Suddenly a man like no other called to them and said to follow Him.

Jesus had been in Galilee preaching the kingdom of God, and very likely John recognized him. Regardless, when this man Jesus called, there was nothing for John to do but follow. He immediately dropped what he was doing and went to Jesus. There is not even record of him saying goodbye to his father. From that point forward, John's life was bound to Jesus.

Jesus later said that anyone who would be His disciple must give up everything they have (Luke 14:33). John did just that—and what a gatherer of souls he became. John serves as an example to us even today. What people or things do we hold dear? Would we give them up in order to gain Jesus?

CAIN: The First "Drip" in the Flood

*Then the L*ORD *said to Cain, "Why are you angry?*
Why is your face downcast? If you do what is right,
will you not be accepted? But if you do not do what
is right, sin is crouching at your door; it desires
to have you, but you must rule over it."

Genesis 4:6–7 NIV

Can we feel sorry for the man who invented murder?

Sure. Cain probably felt sorry for himself. He was the first child born into mankind's fallen state. He farmed a cursed land. It would have been a difficult life. He might have felt bitter. Perhaps he felt justified in keeping his best produce for himself and offering God the rest.

When God called him on that, Cain lashed out—and killed his brother. The ultimate fruit of his labor turned out to be violent murder. But, up until that moment, and perhaps afterward, he probably felt justified in all he did.

He could have avoided this whole sad situation if he had stopped feeling sorry for himself, stopped thinking it was all about him, and focused on God instead. Two faithful sons of Adam might have established a completely different relationship between humanity and God. The Flood might have been avoided. But Cain felt sorry for himself.

Next time you're feeling sorry for yourself, step away from your "justified" wrath. Think of Cain, think of God, and say, "It's Your plan, Lord, not mine. Help me to understand that clearly."

METHUSELAH: Long Life, Short Obituary

Methuselah lived 969 years, and then he died.

Genesis 5:27 NLT

Methuselah is noted for his lifespan, the longest recorded in the Bible, but little else: he had sons and daughters, lived 969 years, and died. Genesis chapter 5 records the long lives of many of the early patriarchs. Enoch, Methuselah's father, had the shortest life span. Yet he is the only one described as having walked faithfully with God.

Adam lived 930 years and was still alive at the birth of Methuselah. Did Adam talk to Methuselah and confess his and Eve's role in the fall? Did Methuselah listen to Adam's description of his walks in the Garden with God? Adam or Enoch, Methuselah's father, must have told him that failing to follow God's direction would eventually lead to disaster.

A long lifespan gives a person ample time to improve his life or sink deeper into sin. With such a long life, did Methuselah pray every day to become a better person? Or, did he plot how to achieve his own selfish desires? Apparently many of his generation chose the latter because "everything they thought or imagined was consistently and totally evil" (Genesis 6:5 NLT).

Whether a person has a long life or one cut short, the goal every day should be to draw closer to God and walk more perfectly in His way.

ABEDNEGO: No Compromise, No Matter What

"If we are thrown into the blazing furnace, the God we serve is able to deliver us from it, and he will deliver us from Your Majesty's hand. But even if he does not. . . we will not serve your gods or worship the image of gold you have set up."

Daniel 3:17–18 NIV

Modern thinking holds that compromise is always a virtue, that holding so strongly to any conviction or belief that you won't bend a little brands you as "narrow minded," "unbending," or "intolerant." (The list goes on!)

The world today probably wouldn't think much of Shadrach, Meshach, and Abednego, three young Hebrew men who served in the court of Nebuchadnezzar, the king of the Babylonian Empire.

These men held a special place in the kingdom, right up until the moment they refused a "bow or die" order straight from the king himself. How did they respond? *We won't bow to your idols, even if it means being burned to a crisp in your furnace.*

Abednego and his two young friends knew full well that their God was more than able to save them from death at the hands of Nebuchadnezzar's men. But they also knew that whether or not God saved them, they would never dishonor Him or defile themselves by bending the knee to the king's golden idol.

Life is filled with situations where compromise is the wiser choice. But when compromise means that God is dishonored, when it means putting His standards in second place, then "we won't bow" should be our response.

JUDAH: A Flawed Instrument of God

The sons of Leah: Reuben the firstborn of Jacob,
Simeon, Levi, Judah, Issachar and Zebulun.
Genesis 35:23 NIV

As the fourth-born son of Jacob and Leah, Judah probably didn't have any hope of inheriting what Reuben would have been entitled to as the firstborn. But when Reuben slept with his father's concubine (verse 22) and Simeon and Levi massacred the men of Shechem (Genesis 34), Judah ended up first in line for the blessing (Genesis 49:8–12).

That didn't stop him from making a string of poor decisions though. He married an ungodly Canaanite woman, Shua, and fathered three children with her: Er, Onan, and Shelah. He went on to choose a Canaanite wife for Er, a woman named Tamar.

Er was so wicked that God took his life. And after God took Onan's life as well, Judah visited a woman he believed to be a harlot—who turned out to be Tamar in disguise. After finding out that Tamar was pregnant, Judah threatened to have her burned before finally acknowledging the child was his (Genesis 38).

In spite of the mess Judah created, God brought forth the Messiah through the line of Perez—one of the twins Tamar bore (Matthew 1:3, Luke 3:33).

While God never promises to remove the ramifications of sin, He can redeem situations and people that we would think beyond hope.

CALEB: Ten Angry Men

*And Caleb stilled the people before Moses, and said,
Let us go up at once, and possess it; for we are well able
to overcome it. But the men that went up with
him said, We be not able to go up against the
people; for they are stronger than we.*

Numbers 13:30–31 KJV

They had arrived at the border of the Promised Land, and Moses sent twelve tribal leaders to explore it. Ten of them said, in effect, "It's a wonderful place, but scary! We should go elsewhere."

Two men, Caleb and Joshua, declared that the Israelites could conquer it.

All twelve had scouted the same land. Ten seemed to have returned in fear. God Himself said Caleb had a different spirit. He knew God had promised them the land, so what did he have to fear? Not the Canaanites—and not the other spies.

Caleb's example encouraged Joshua. A young aide to Moses, he had already led the Israelites in battle. He would go on to become one of Israel's greatest heroes and one of God's most faith-filled servants.

Were the others impressed? Not really. . .they wanted to stone the two brave men (Numbers 14:10). However, God rewarded Joshua and Caleb by letting them enter the Promised Land, while all the others died in the wilderness.

How much courage does it take to stand against your peers? A lot. But if you're standing with God, the example you set will be more powerful than you could possibly imagine.

What Did That Man's Name Mean?

Just as today, some biblical names had meanings.
Here are a few of those meanings,
including names of some men in this book.

ABRAHAM: Father of a multitude

ABRAM: High father

ABSALOM: Friendly

ADAM: Ruddy

AGABUS: Locust

AGRIPPA: Wild horse tamer

AHAB: Friend of his father

AHIMELECH: Brother of the king

ANANIAS: God has favored

ANDREW: Manly

APOLLOS: The sun

AQUILA: Eagle

JOSEPH OF ARIMATHEA:
A Secret Admirer

Now Joseph was a disciple of Jesus,
but secretly because he feared the Jewish leaders.
John 19:38 NIV

Everything we know about Joseph of Arimathea comes from just a handful of verses in each Gospel. He was a rich man who had become a disciple of Jesus (Matthew 27:57), a prominent member of the Sanhedrin (Mark 15:43), a good and upright man who had not consented to the Sanhedrin's decision to crucify Jesus (Luke 23:50–51), and a man who kept his devotion to Jesus a secret (John 19:38). This was an unusual combination of traits in Joseph's time.

Jesus had taught how hard it was for a rich man to enter heaven, yet here was one who had given his heart to Him. On top of that, this rich man was also a member of the Sanhedrin, the very council that condemned Jesus to death. It's no wonder Joseph kept his true beliefs a secret; it would have been scandalous had the Sanhedrin found out, not to mention a danger to Joseph's life.

However, there can be no doubt about Joseph's devotion to Jesus in the end. After Jesus' death, Joseph personally petitioned for the body, prepared it with expensive perfume, and laid it in his own tomb. He sacrificed material goods and risked his position and standing in order to honor the King of kings.

SAMSON: Sort of Set Apart

When her son was born, she named him Samson.
And the LORD blessed him as he grew up.

Judges 13:24 NLT

There were no cell phones in the years before Samson's birth. The Internet would not be available for a few dozen centuries. So God chose an angel to personally deliver a message to a couple who hadn't been able to have children. The message to mom was simple: "You will soon become pregnant and give birth to a son" (Judges 13:3 NLT). Samson would become the most famous Nazirite in the Old Testament, and he would be visibly different from his peers.

To be a Nazirite meant to be set apart. They had restrictions on what they could eat and drink. They followed laws that forbade them to cut their hair. In Samson's case, his visible gift was incredible strength. However, just because his body was "set apart" didn't mean that Samson was internally fortified with virtue and character.

The Philistines were the enemies of the Israelites, but when it came time for Samson to marry, he saw a Philistine woman who "looked good." Reluctantly, his parents arranged the marriage, and before he ever met Delilah, this impulsive strongman experienced the sting of a woman's betrayal.

Setting ourselves apart has to be about more than how we *look* to others. When our hearts are set apart, the internal change will produce far greater results than merely going through outward motions.

ISHMAEL: God Doesn't Forget the Outcasts

*And God heard the voice of the lad; and the angel of God
called to Hagar out of heaven, and said unto her,
What aileth thee, Hagar? fear not; for God
hath heard the voice of the lad where he is.*

Genesis 21:17 KJV

No one gets to choose anything about his birth.

After Ishmael's birth was arranged by Abram's wife, Sarai, God told his Egyptian mother, Hagar, that Ishmael would live without the support of human society and that he would produce twelve sons who would become leaders. God also said Ishmael would live to the east of his brothers and that he would be at odds with everyone.

When Ishmael was a young teenager, he and Hagar were sent packing because of what today might be seen as a typical behavior of mocking his little brother.

After they ran out of water and Hagar expected they would die, God intervened to show her a nearby well and promised that Ishmael would be the father of a great nation.

Then we are told that Ishmael went on to become an archer, and that his mother took a wife for him from the Egyptians.

Someone must have taught him archery, since the bows of that time and place were complex weapons. And, if he lived by his archery, he must have learned to hunt. Ishmael didn't give up on life, even though he had become an outcast. Why? Because "God was with the lad" (Genesis 21:20 KJV).

JOSHUA: The Faithful Aide

The LORD said to Moses, "Come up to me on the mountain and stay here, and I will give you the tablets of stone with the law and commandments I have written for their instruction." Then Moses set out with Joshua his aide, and Moses went up on the mountain of God.

Exodus 24:12–13 NIV

You're a captain-general of the Hebrews under Moses—his right-hand man—when your commander tells you he wants you to accompany him up to the holy mountain of God, where God will supply the stone tablets containing His law.

Scary?

You bet. But as frightening as it would be to approach such a powerful God, going right up to the cloud in which He appears, what does the invitation to accompany Moses say about Joshua's character? A lot!

One day, Joshua, the son of Nun, would become Moses' successor, but not yet. In this moment, his duty was to support Moses as the leader of God's people. He had exhibited his faithfulness in the past by fighting (and defeating) the Amalekites, just as Moses had ordered (Exodus 17:9). Now here he was—closer in proximity to God than any other man except Moses.

Are you second (or third, or fourth) in command at work, or church, or in your small group? Are you fully supportive of the person God has put in charge for this particular season, always faithful to help carry out the vision God has given? If so, God will bless you, too.

ABEL: Nice Guys Finish Last?

Abel also brought an offering–fat portions from some of the firstborn of his flock. The LORD looked with favor on Abel and his offering, but on Cain and his offering he did not look with favor. So Cain was very angry, and his face was downcast.

Genesis 4:4-5 NIV

You might be tempted to think, from the story of Abel and his brother Cain, that "nice guys finish last." But if that's what you think, then you're mistaken.

Abel, second son of Adam and Eve, was the family "good boy." He may have consistently done what his parents asked. Certainly he loved God deeply, for when it came time to make an offering, he brought his heavenly Father the best he had. And God smiled on him.

Cain, the elder son, may have thought, *Mom always loved you best—and Dad does, too. Now even God is taking your side.* Quickly, sibling rivalry overcame brotherly love. Feeling unloved and unaccepted because God knew that his sacrifice wasn't from the heart, Cain took out his anger on his brother. As a result, he committed the first murder in history and was condemned to wander the earth for the rest of his days.

Abel didn't have a long life, but judging from the joy that accompanied his sacrifice to God, it was a successful one. Jesus commended Abel as a righteous man (Matthew 23:35). Though Cain lived on for many more barren years after killing his brother, who will say that those years of life were better? No one.

If finishing last means joy in eternity, maybe being last is the first thing we should aim for.

THE HEALED LEPER:
A Thankful Man Returns

One of them, when he saw he was healed, came back,
praising God in a loud voice. He threw himself at
Jesus' feet and thanked him—and he was a Samaritan.

Luke 17:15-16 NIV

The band of ten lepers in Luke 17 had multiple strikes against them before their encounter with Jesus. First, as lepers they were obligated by Moses' Law (Leviticus 13:46) to keep their distance from everyone else. And second, at least one of them was a Samaritan, and Samaritans had a strained relationship with Jews for a number of reasons— they were racially mixed and their religion was both different and deficient.

But Jesus never recoiled over physical or spiritual impurities. As the ten lepers saw Him coming, they cried out for mercy and He granted it to them, healing all ten. The one who was identified as a Samaritan returned to thank Jesus, but the other nine did not. While Jesus expressed disappointment, going so far as to ask the Samaritan, "Where are the other nine?" (v. 17), His compassion for them hadn't been conditional, nor was it dependent on how grateful they would be in response to His granting their healing.

Yet, how often is our willingness to show compassion to castoffs conditional, based on our perception of their worth or a perceived future response to our action? What if we cared less about their response and more about their souls?

JONAH: Overconfident in God?

"I knew that you are a gracious and compassionate God,
slow to anger and abounding in love, a God who
relents from sending calamity."

Jonah 4:2 NIV

Jonah had great confidence in God's mercies, but he didn't *want* God to have mercy! Most of us know the story of Jonah: how God told him to go to Nineveh and preach against the Ninevites' wickedness, how Jonah fled in the opposite direction, and how he ended up in the belly of a great fish. But do we remember *why* Jonah disobeyed God?

Chapter 4 of the book of Jonah tells us that he disobeyed God because he *knew* God would have mercy on the Ninevites if they repented, and Jonah thought that wasn't right. He thought the Ninevites deserved punishment, and he tried to withhold the Word of God to ensure that judgment came.

Are you a modern day Jonah? When you see the people around you—at work, at the grocery store, in your neighborhood—do you see Ninevites who should be punished, or a field ripe for harvest? Do you go out of your way, even out of your comfort zone, to bring in the harvest?

God desires to gather for Himself a people from every nation, tribe, people, and language (Revelation 7:9), and He has instructed us to go to those people and proclaim the Gospel (Mark 16:15). Do you have enough love to do His will?

THE CENTURION:
Between Heaven and Earth

*When Jesus heard these things, he marvelled at him, and turned
him about, and said unto the people that followed him, I say
unto you, I have not found so great faith, no, not in Israel.
And they that were sent, returning to the house,
found the servant whole that had been sick.*

Luke 7:9–10 KJV

The centurion did an extraordinary thing. In effect, he prayed
to Jesus while the Lord still walked the earth as a man!

We might petition God for help or healing through
heartfelt prayers sent heavenward. We trust they will be
answered, but we don't expect God to turn up personally in
all His glory. He doesn't need to. We have faith in His power
regardless.

After his initial message, the centurion sent a postscript
affirming that Jesus didn't have to attend in person. He just
had to say the word. The centurion had a faith that impressed
even Jesus.

But he had more than that. He recognized the power
of God *and* he recognized his own unworthiness. He was
deemed "worthy" by his Jewish neighbors because he loved
their nation and had built a synagogue, but he himself had a
humbler view of his standing. Nevertheless, he trusted that
God could and would act powerfully on his behalf.

In the book of Mark, Jesus tells us to love God and our
neighbor. If you ever wondered where best to stand to do
both those things, stand where the centurion stood.

REUBEN: Part-Time Integrity

When Reuben returned to the cistern and saw
that Joseph was not there, he tore his clothes.

Genesis 37:29 NIV

It was a sibling rivalry gone too far. Joseph arrived to check up on ten of his brothers and then report back to their dad. Joseph had already given their father, Jacob, a bad report and the brothers had apparently decided to prevent his next bad report by murdering him.

Reuben suggested they toss him in a pit. He planned to come back and rescue the boy, but while he was away his brothers took Joseph's coat, dipped it in goat's blood, and sold Joseph to a caravan of Ishmaelite slave traders. The brothers then took the bloodied garment back to Dad and fabricated the story of his death.

Reuben was likely filled with regret for many years. He and his brothers wouldn't tell their dad the truth until they discovered Joseph alive in Egypt many years later.

While Reuben wanted to do the right thing and save Joseph, he also had significant sin baggage. He had committed adultery with one of his father's concubines. Consistently doing the right thing seemed impossible for him. His father, Jacob, described Reuben as "unstable as water" (Genesis 49:4 KJV). Reuben struggled to maintain his integrity.

God wants all of us to finish well (2 Timothy 4:7). As firstborn, Reuben demonstrated a sense of responsibility. However, we find no record that Reuben walked steadfastly with God.

GIDEON: Reluctant Leader Surprised

"Pardon me, my lord," Gideon replied, "but how can I save Israel? My clan is the weakest in Manasseh, and I am the least in my family."

Judges 6:15 NIV

Gideon had no faith that the God of Moses would remove the Midianite oppression from Israel. When the angel of the Lord addressed him as a mighty man of valor, Gideon's response could be paraphrased: "Oh, sure. Think about it. My family is powerless and I'm the weakest. And our fathers told us God brought us out of Egypt, but where is He now?"

The Lord said He would be with Gideon, and he would triumph over the Midianites. Gideon wasn't convinced. He asked for a sign that would prove that it was God speaking to him. When Gideon prepared a meal, the angel of the Lord had him place the meat and bread on a stone. The angel then touched the end of his staff to the meat, and fire came from the stone and burned up the meal.

The Lord then told Gideon to take his father's bull, pull down the family altar to Baal, cut down the trees associated with it, build an altar to God, and sacrifice the bull on it. Gideon and ten servants did the job at night to avoid the wrath of his father and the local men.

But in the morning, his father took his side and told the men they should let Baal defend himself, if he was indeed a god.

It surprised Gideon that God had chosen him, but when God does something, He uses whomever He chooses!

What Did That Man's Name Mean?

Just as today, some biblical names had meanings.
Here are a few of those meanings,
including names of some men in this book.

BAAL: Master

BAKBAKKAR: Searcher

BALAAM: Foreigner

BALAK: Waster

BARABBAS: Son of abba (father)

BARAK: Lightning

BARNABAS: Son of consolation

BARTIMAEUS: Son of Timaeus

BARUCH: Blessed

BARZILLAI: Iron-hearted

BENJAMIN: Son of the right hand

BUKKI: Wasteful

NAAMAN: To Bow to Rimmon

*"When my master the king goes into the temple of the god
Rimmon to worship there and leans on my arm,
may the LORD pardon me when I bow, too."*

2 Kings 5:18 NLT

Naaman, a Syrian commander, had leprosy. An Israelite
servant girl said the prophet Elisha could cure him of his
disease.

When Naaman traveled to Israel, Elisha sent a
messenger out with instructions for him to wash in the Jordan
seven times. At first, Naaman rejected Elisha's commands.
Wouldn't Syrian rivers do? His servants convinced him to
act as ordered, however, and Naaman was healed.

Naaman asked Elisha for a load of soil to take home to
stand upon as he sacrificed to no other god but the Lord.
He did have a question though. His duties required him
to assist his master in worshipping the false god Rimmon.
When his master leaned on Naaman's arm to bow, Naaman
was expected to bow, too. Would God pardon this?

Naaman wanted a firm answer one way or the other.
Instead, Elisha told him to "go in peace." Like Christians
today, Naaman would have to seek the answer in prayer
to his newly-found God. (After his decision, it seems that
Naaman lost his position, because Syria was soon at war with
Israel again.) By reading the Bible with a determination to
find the truth, praying in sincerity, and listening to the Holy
Spirit, the answer that reflects the will of God will become
apparent.

JOSIAH: The Eight-Year-Old King

*Josiah was eight years old when he became king, and he
reigned in Jerusalem thirty-one years. His mother's name
was Jedidah daughter of Adaiah; she was from Bozkath.*

2 Kings 22:1 NIV

Okay, admit it. Every time you read this passage that
describes Judah's king as an eight-year-old boy, you envision
a toy truck in his hand—or, if you're more literal, you see a
typical young boy who has no concept of patience, sacrifice,
or humility, all of which are major character traits of a good
ruler.

So how in the world could an eight-year-old boy lead a
nation the way Josiah did—becoming one of the best kings
that God's people would ever serve under, bringing about
godly reforms to the entire nation?

We know that his father, King Amon, was a wicked
king who followed in his father's (King Manasseh) idol-
worshipping footsteps and was eventually murdered. As
such, Amon certainly didn't provide Josiah with proper
spiritual guidance. We know less about Josiah's mother,
Jedidah daughter of Adaiah, but some believe she must have
been a godly woman who quietly guided Josiah in the ways
of the Lord.

Maybe the old saying, "Behind every great man, is a
great woman," applied in this case.

Do you listen to the godly women God has placed in
your life?

ABRAHAM: Taking the First Step

The LORD had said to Abram, "Go from your country,
your people and your father's household to the land I will
show you. . . . So Abram went, as the LORD had told him.

Genesis 12:1, 4 NIV

God made Abraham (then called Abram) some amazing promises when He instructed him to leave Harran. Who wouldn't want the Creator of the universe Himself to promise greatness, blessings, protection, and an opportunity to bless every nation on earth?

But in Genesis 12:1–4, you'll notice that God didn't provide Abraham much in the way of details—even where he would be going and what route he would take to get there (also see Hebrews 11:8). He simply told Abraham to pack up his family and "go from your country."

If we're honest, we'd have to admit that when God communicates a vision, we're more prone to want to see a travel plan, an itinerary, and a spreadsheet before we take that first step of obedience. It's human nature to want details before we step out.

But as we read some of the biblical accounts of God communicating with His people, we see that He doesn't always provide a lot of details ahead of time. Rather, He just tells them, "Get up and go!"

God may have communicated His vision for you, and He may have given you some first small steps in making that vision a reality. But don't worry if He hasn't filled in a lot of the details. Just trust Him and follow Him step by step. He'll never let you down or fail to keep every one of His promises.

JOSEPH: Trusting the Promise of God

*Then Joseph said to his brothers, "I am about to die. But God
will surely come to your aid and take you up out of this land
to the land he promised on oath to Abraham, Isaac and Jacob."
And Joseph made the Israelites swear an oath and said,
"God will surely come to your aid, and then you
must carry my bones up from this place."*

Genesis 50:24–25 NIV

Joseph spent most of his life in Egypt, far from the land that
God had promised to his father, Jacob; yet at his deathbed,
at the age of 110 years, Joseph was confident that God
would bring His people back to the Promised Land. How
did Joseph have such faith? Perhaps because he experienced
God's work firsthand multiple times.

God had raised Joseph from slavery to prosperity as a
servant of the captain of Pharaoh's guard. God later raised
Joseph from prison to become the second most powerful
man in Egypt. Joseph had been in hard places before, but he
had seen how God was faithful. So at his deathbed, Joseph
fully expected God to be faithful to His promises to his
forefathers.

While God promises many blessings to believers, He
doesn't say our life on this earth will be easy. In fact, the
Bible teaches that believers will experience troubles and even
persecution. No matter how difficult life may be though, we
can rest assured that "in all things God works for the good
of those who love him" (Romans 8:28 NIV). God is with us
even in times of trials, and He will be faithful.

CORNELIUS: Opening the Door for the Rest of the World

While Peter yet spake these words, the Holy Ghost fell on all them which heard the word. And they of the circumcision which believed were astonished, as many as came with Peter, because that on the Gentiles also was poured out the gift of the Holy Ghost.

Acts 10:44–45 KJV

Those of us who aren't Jewish Christians owe a huge debt of gratitude to a man we might rarely think about.

Jesus had commanded His disciples to preach the Gospel to people of every nation (Mark 16:15), but after His resurrection the disciples took a while to actually do that. In the meantime, faith was taking root in the hearts of the most unlikely people.

Cornelius of Caesarea was a centurion in the occupying Roman army. He had devoted his heart to God and was well respected among the Jews, but he was a Gentile. The disciples—all Jewish—didn't really know what to do with a man like that. But God did. He sent a vision to Peter declaring that the old ideas of "clean" and "unclean" people had no place in His new kingdom. The Gentiles were to be welcomed in. In other words, Jesus loved the whole world!

At the same time God told Cornelius to seek out Peter. The result was the first Gentile baptism.

Cornelius couldn't possibly have imagined how God would use him. None of us can. But he believed and obeyed anyway, and so should we.

THE RICH YOUNG RULER:
Good-Guy Checklist

*Jesus answered, "If you want to be perfect, go,
sell your possessions and give to the poor, and you
will have treasure in heaven. Then come, follow me."*

Matthew 19:21 NIV

On the religious scale of goodness, the rich young ruler seemed to be off the charts. He must have had a priority "good guy" checklist, and he was committed to marking off each accomplishment. When he heard about Jesus, he may have believed this teacher might have a few more merit badges he could acquire, thinking they might bring perfection and right standing before God. Plus, others would be impressed.

When he heard Jesus' response, though, he left saddened. Maybe he thought following Jesus was just too high a price to pay. He had proven he could juggle a lot of outward religious deeds, but taking that next step was something he ultimately wouldn't do. He loved his riches—and the luxuries and comforts they afforded—too much.

By placing possessions over relationship the rich young ruler left heavyhearted. Did he realize that what he owned had become the objects of worship for him? Did he understand that all the outward signs he was quick to demonstrate came up short? Was the commitment to follow too much?

When confronted with truth, we all have a choice to make. When Jesus says, "Come, follow me," may we see the value in that relationship and wholeheartedly follow.

HEZEKIAH: Following God's Path

*He in the first year of his reign, in the first month,
opened the doors of the house of the LORD, and repaired them.*

2 Chronicles 29:3 KJV

Hezekiah's father, Ahaz, was a horrible example. After being defeated in battle, he decided the gods of the enemy had brought them victory. So he set up altars to those gods all over Judah.

But when Hezekiah became king at the age of twenty-five, he immediately turned the hearts of his people toward the true God. Beginning with repairing the temple doors, he put the Levites to work cleaning the neglected place of worship and restoring its furnishings to their former splendor.

He gathered the rulers of Jerusalem to the temple to offer a sacrifice. Many came to see and take part in the worship that centered on a burnt offering and was accompanied by singing and the playing of musical instruments.

Later, Hezekiah sent messages throughout the land that all should come to Jerusalem to keep the Passover, which had not been observed for a long time. The joy that flowed during these celebrations released the nations' suppressed longing to be in fellowship with their God.

Hezekiah's leadership freed his subjects' spirits to publicly worship after years of idolatry. . .and he didn't order a survey to see what course of action would make him most popular.

MOSES: The Shepherd

But Moses protested to God, "Who am I to appear before Pharaoh? Who am I to lead the people of Israel out of Egypt?"
Exodus 3:11 NLT

After being raised in Pharaoh's palace, Moses fled Egypt because he killed an Egyptian who had been beating a Hebrew slave. Moses escaped to Midian. While he rested by a well, seven sisters came to water their flock, but other shepherds drove them away. Moses rescued the women and watered their flock. Later on he married one of the daughters and became a shepherd.

Whatever skills Moses had learned in Egypt were eclipsed by those needed to be a shepherd: leading, protecting, feeding, watering, shearing, delivering lambs, and finding lost sheep. Moving the flock from one grazing area to another required that he set a pace that the weakest, slowest member of the flock could manage.

Moses was tending sheep when he saw the burning bush and received the commission to tell Pharaoh to let the Hebrew slaves go. The skills and patience Moses learned in the forty years of tending sheep may not have prepared him for freeing the children of Israel, but they certainly prepared him for leading them in the wilderness for the next forty years.

A Christian's life may move forward as straight as an arrow to the goal God has set for him. But often there are fits and starts, and only in hindsight does a Christian realize that, like Moses, God has been preparing him to accomplish a specific task.

JUDAS: Not Iscariot

When they arrived, they went upstairs to the room where they
were staying. Those present were Peter, John, James and Andrew;
Philip and Thomas, Bartholomew and Matthew; James son of
Alphaeus and Simon the Zealot, and Judas son of James.

Acts 1:13 NIV

Ever wished you had a different name? Imagine how Judas, the apostle (whom scripture also refers to as Lebbaeus, Thaddaeus, and Judas son of James) must have felt after Judas Iscariot betrayed Jesus for thirty pieces of silver.

Even now, as we read the Bible and come across the name of Judas, we automatically think of Iscariot. The Gospel of John (14:22) refers to the apostle as "Judas" and immediately adds the words "not Iscariot" for the sake of clarity.

While we don't know a lot about this particular Judas, one commentator says he "held but a low place among the apostles." But even so, he was among those who traveled back to the upper room after the ascension of Jesus, where Acts 1:14 says they were of one accord in devoting themselves to prayer, knowing that Christ had commissioned them to take the Gospel to the ends of the earth.

Tradition holds that Judas went on to preach the Gospel far and wide, all the while appearing to be content to live in the shadows of some of the other apostles. How comfortable are you with serving without public recognition if that is the lot God has assigned you?

ABRAHAM: The Persistent Intercession

The men turned away and went toward Sodom,
but Abraham remained standing before the LORD.

Genesis 18:22 NIV

Abraham didn't like what God had just told him. The sin in the city of Sodom had reached such a grievous level that God intended to destroy the city. But instead of giving up on Sodom, where his nephew Lot and his family lived, Abraham began what can only be seen as bargaining with God for the city's destiny.

Abraham's prayer of intercession began with him pleading with God to spare Sodom on account of fifty righteous people. From there, he asked God if He would have mercy on the city for forty-five righteous people...then forty...then thirty-five...then thirty...then twenty...then finally ten.

From a human perspective, it's easy for us to wonder if God might have grown impatient with Abraham's haggling. But He didn't. In fact, He assured Abraham that He would indeed spare the city if just ten righteous people could be found there. In doing so, He showed that He wants His people to intercede on behalf of others.

Intercession is a special kind of prayer. It's opening your heart and "standing in the gap" (Ezekiel 22:30) for someone—and doing it consistently and persistently until you see results. But here's the wonderful truth about this kind of prayer: God loves hearing it, loves answering it, and is in no way put off when we refuse to quit until we receive our answer.

What Did That Man's Name Mean?

Just as today, some biblical names had meanings.
Here are a few of those meanings,
including names of some men in this book.

CAIAPHAS: The dell

CAIN: Lance

CALEB: Forcible

CANAAN: Humiliated

CAREAH: Bald

CARMI: Gardener

CARPUS: Fruit

CEPHAS: The rock

CLEOPAS: Renowned father

COZ: Thorn

CRISPUS: Crisp

CUSHI: A Cushite

DANIEL: Doing Things God's Way

But Daniel purposed in his heart that he would not defile himself with the portion of the king's meat, nor with the wine which he drank: therefore he requested of the prince of the eunuchs that he might not defile himself.

Daniel 1:8 KJV

Some guys just seem to ask for trouble.

When the Jewish people were taken into captivity by the Babylonians, Daniel, as a young nobleman, had an opportunity to help himself. He was among the group selected to be taught the ways of the Babylonian court. It was to be an integration of the most comfortable sort. The young nobles would become as Babylonians and their captors could say, "Look how well we treat them!"

But Daniel, Hananiah, and Mishael, who could have settled for a life of luxury, chose to keep their integrity. At each step they were decried by enemies. Time and again they held to their faith, even when it seemed they would die because of it. But all three continued to prosper. Daniel became a powerful man and a positive influence on four different kings.

His captors—Nebuchadnezzar, Belshazzar, Darius, and Cyrus—were each in their time the most powerful men on earth. They weren't guys you wanted to annoy, but Daniel wasn't really looking for trouble. He was just more concerned for his soul than his life, which meant no one but God had any power over him. And God used that power to deliver him!

JOHN: A Not-So-Humble Apostle?

*"Let one of us sit at your right and the other
at your left in your glory."*

Mark 10:37 NIV

John, son of Zebedee and disciple of Jesus, had just heard Jesus say that no one who had left everything in order to follow Him would fail "to receive a hundred times as much in this present age. . .and in the age to come eternal life" (Mark 10:30 NIV). That apparently wasn't good enough for John and his brother James though, because just a little later, the two asked to sit in the places of highest honor at Jesus' side in His glory.

Apparently it wasn't enough to receive blessings; they wanted more than others. One can't help but wonder if the brothers would have argued about who got to sit on Jesus' right side if He had granted their original request!

John's behavior shows just how strong our self-interest can be. We receive but want more—not because we're trying to draw closer to Christ, but rather because we're trying to satisfy ourselves with things other than Christ.

The Christian life is one of continued battle against sin and selfishness, and alongside the promise of blessings in Mark 10:30, Jesus said believers would also receive persecution. Fortunately, believers have the assurance of ultimate victory in Christ. He is our one true need. Pray that God will show you that your ultimate satisfaction is in Christ.

SAUL: Israel's First, Impetuous King

*Saul was thirty years old when he became king,
and he reigned over Israel forty-two years.*

1 Samuel 13:1 NIV

There is basic information about Saul—such as the fact that his dad's name was Kish, he was handsome and tall, and he chose to hide among the luggage. Then there are revealing moments that help us see Israel's first king for who he really was.

One of the reasons the Bible is filled with stories is so we can identify with the humanity of people whom God either used or whom He wants us to view as cautionary examples of what behaviors and choices we should avoid.

Saul didn't ask to be king and tried to avoid being publicly selected, but once he became king he was willing to contemplate murder to stay in his position. He made David a leader, yet tried to kill him when he learned that David had been chosen king. Saul put laws in place that outlawed the use of mediums, yet when he didn't know what to do, he sought a medium to speak to the prophet Samuel. He often made decisions without asking God for help.

Is Saul so different from us? We fight to stay in control. We occasionally commit sin in ways that we usually condemn. We find it easy to make fun of the successes of others in an effort to damage their credibility. We have decisions to make, but refuse to follow God's plain counsel. Who knew we had so much in common?

HUSHAI: David's Double Agent

And Hushai said unto Absalom, Nay; but whom the L<small>ORD</small>,
and this people, and all the men of Israel, choose,
his will I be, and with him will I abide.

2 Samuel 16:18 KJV

God has not told us to imitate every example found in His Word. Sometimes the Bible simply describes what happened. Hushai's story merits a close look and careful thought.

At David's bidding, his friend pledged to be an advisor and counselor to David's usurper son Absalom. He told Absalom he would serve whomever the Lord and the men of Israel chose. That would seem to be dishonest, since his loyalty remained with David. Hushai did give Absalom advice that could have worked against David, and because he knew the Lord had chosen David, he was speaking the truth in his pledge to serve God's choice. He was less than forthright, but honest.

Hushai then sent word to David to go with his men across the Jordan out of Absalom's path. In that, he proved his worth to David.

That's the last we hear of Hushai. It's less than clear whether his behavior is exemplary. We aren't told in this story or anywhere else in the Bible that deception is allowed as long as it's not an outright lie. We're not required to always tell everything we know, but we're not to encourage anyone to believe what is untrue either.

MOSES: Interviewed for Greatness

"My grace is all you need. My power works best in weakness."
2 Corinthians 12:9 NLT

A potential employee is being interviewed for a job, and the employee's first question is, "Who are you?" He then asks the manager, "Who am I?" When told he would be a salesman, the candidate asks, "What if the customers don't believe me?" He also confesses, "I'm a person with poor speaking skills." As the interview concludes, he says, "Why don't you hire someone else?"

Such an employee would hardly get a callback interview. But during God's conversation with Moses at the burning bush, Moses asked similar questions (Exodus 3:1–22, 4:1–17). He must have rejoiced when God said He would rescue His people from oppression in Egypt. But Moses was dismayed when he learned that he would be the one to challenge Pharaoh and lead the people out of slavery.

Forty years had passed since Moses had fled Egypt. He'd made a new life for himself in Midian. He was so far removed from his people that he hadn't circumcised his own son (Exodus 4:25). At first, he resisted his call to greatness. God overcame all of Moses' objections one by one, and sent him toward Egypt to his appointment with destiny. Moses learned that God equips a person to carry out an assignment. It's as true today as it was in Moses' day.

JOSHUA: The Faithful Leader

Then the LORD said to Joshua, "See, I have delivered Jericho into your hands, along with its king and its fighting men."

Joshua 6:2 NIV

Having been commissioned by God to take the Promised Land as Israel's rightful inheritance, you are near a locked-down Jericho (Joshua 6:1–2) pondering your next move. Suddenly a heavenly being—the commander of God's army—appears and tells you he has delivered the city into your hands. He goes on to give you specific marching orders about how to take the city and the plan works exactly the way he says it will.

This is what Joshua, the son of Nun, experienced as he transitioned from the faithful aide to Moses to the faithful leader of Israel who listened to God. He didn't question God's plan for taking Jericho, even though marching around the city for seven days might have seemed like an odd thing to do. He didn't run ahead of God, charging the city gates when God had other plans. Instead, he obeyed God's instructions and the city walls fell.

Are you currently dealing with a coworker who is assassinating your character or a friend who has taken advantage of you in some way and has become a foe? Don't run ahead of God in your own strength, but rather trust Him to show you the solution.

ABRAHAM: An Example of Great Faith

By faith Abraham, when God tested him, offered Isaac as a sacrifice. He who had embraced the promises was about to sacrifice his one and only son, even though God had said to him, "It is through Isaac that your offspring will be reckoned."

Hebrews 11:17–18 NIV

Other than Moses, no character from the Old Testament receives more New Testament ink than Abraham. With the life of faith Abraham lived, it's no wonder that the New Testament had so much to say about the father of Israel.

The New Testament reports that by faith, Abraham did the following:

- obeyed God and left to settle in the Promised Land, even though he had no idea where he was going (Hebrews 11:8–9).
- became a parent of a promised son, even though he and his wife were both well beyond childbearing years (Hebrews 11:11–12).
- passed God's test of his devotion to Him (Hebrews 11:17–19).
- was declared righteous before God and called God's friend (James 2:23).

God inspired the writers of the New Testament books to focus on Abraham simply because He wants to encourage us to live a life with the faith Abraham demonstrated over and over again.

Abraham's faith inspired Him to trust in the One he knew was faithful in keeping His promises. While Abraham wasn't a perfect man, he shows us what a man who takes God at His word can accomplish.

JONAH: Of Fish and Jesus

"This is a wicked generation. It asks for a sign, but none will be given it except the sign of Jonah. For as Jonah was a sign to the Ninevites, so also will the Son of Man be to this generation."

Luke 11:29–30 NIV

When certain people asked Jesus for a sign, Jesus referred to the "sign of Jonah." Jonah was a prophet in Israel before or during the reign of Jeroboam II. God called Jonah to go to the city of Nineveh and preach against the residents' wickedness, but Jonah disobeyed God and tried to flee in a ship. Because of his disobedience, Jonah ended up thrown into the sea and swallowed by a great fish, where he remained for three days. During that time, Jonah called upon God and appealed to Him for salvation. God heard his prayers and after three days caused the fish to cast Jonah upon dry land.

This was the sign Jesus repeated, though it was through His humble obedience in contrast to Jonah's disobedience. Jesus offered Himself as a sacrifice in order to save many. He was beaten, crucified, and laid in a tomb for three days, and after those three days, God raised Him from the dead.

What a comfort for believers to know that when we're disobedient, we can still rest in Christ's obedience. When Jonah finally went to Nineveh and testified, the people repented and were saved. May we also obey God and be used for His purposes.

CYRUS: School's Out. . .
Time to Go Home

Thus saith Cyrus king of Persia, The LORD God of heaven hath given me all the kingdoms of the earth; and he hath charged me to build him an house at Jerusalem, which is in Judah.

Ezra 1:2 KJV

Did King Cyrus know God? Not really, but he had at least a passing acquaintance. However, God knew King Cyrus and used him in a powerful way!

His chosen people had severely tried God's patience so He sent the Babylonians to remind them how much they needed Him. The Jews were taken from their homes, their temple was destroyed, and as a nation they only existed in memory and in exile.

That was the lesson. Now, to see if it had been learned.

Cyrus the Great of Persia eventually swept down from the northeast and conquered the Babylonian empire. One of the first things he did was to declare a general amnesty and tell the captive peoples—including the Jews—that they could go home again. Not only that, but he provided money for rebuilding and let them take the sacred objects that had been looted from the temple.

Now, why would he do that? Surely a king could use all the slaves he could get. But God told Cyrus He had a different plan, and Cyrus obeyed.

When we find ourselves in times of trial, we should learn from it and wait patiently for our "Cyrus." He won't necessarily come in the form we expect, but God will send him.

SAMUEL: A Prophet's Résumé

Then the word of the LORD came to Samuel.
1 Samuel 15:10 NIV

Samuel's birth was an answer to a mother's prayer, and his life was dedicated to the service of God long before he ever took his first breath. As a young boy he served in the temple with Eli, a priest whose reputation was heavily tarnished.

Even though it was rare for God to speak audibly in those days, He called to Samuel in the middle of the night. Once Samuel recognized it was the voice of God he listened to a prophecy against the aging priest. The next morning Samuel spoke to Eli, not as a boy, but as a prophet.

Samuel's résumé is impressive: he anointed kings, prophesied against rulers, was led by God to understand His Word, and spoke truth when it was unpopular. Samuel was a manly man. His word had impact. Others may have disliked what he said, but the end result was often a message from God that none could argue against.

Samuel's anointing as a prophet was discovered early and was sought often by others. While never a king, he was often sought out as if he were a ruler. He was also sought out by kings. Yet he always sought to serve the King of kings.

Dedicating ourselves to God's will is an important step toward a future less dependent on our own plans and more dependent on His plan for a life of impact.

What Did That Man's Name Mean?

Just as today, some biblical names had meanings.
Here are a few of those meanings,
including names of some men in this book.

DANIEL: Judge of God

DARA: Pearl of knowledge

DAVID: Beloved

DEKAR: Stab

DIBLAIM: Two cakes

DIBRI: Wordy

DIDYMUS: Twin

DISHON: Antelope

DODAI: Sick

DODO: Loving

DOEG: Anxious

DUMAH: Silence

ISAAC: Accepting the Inevitable

Wherefore she [Sarah] said unto Abraham, Cast out this bondwoman and her son: for the son of this bondwoman shall not be heir with my son, even with Isaac.

Genesis 21:10 KJV

Isaac's birth was the fulfillment of God's promise, so his mom always liked him best. When Isaac was very young, his half-brother Ishmael and Ishmael's mother were sent packing. This was to make sure that Isaac got all the inheritance and the powerful promises God had made to his father, Abraham. It might seem he was being spoiled.

In obedience to God, Abraham was willing to kill Isaac as a sacrifice. In the nick of time, however, God provided a ram as a substitute. We have no hint of Isaac's day-to-day life. His mother died when he was thirty-seven, and he mourned her until he married Rebekah when he was forty.

After Sarah's death, Abraham took Keturah as his wife and produced six more sons. But they were not in the will. When they were grown, Abraham gave them parting gifts and sent them away, "eastward."

Isaac was still the favored son. We're not told what effect this had on the other sons, but in that culture sons didn't question a family patriarch's decrees.

When Abraham died at 175 years old, Isaac and Ishmael buried him. That the survivors could cooperate in this seems to show that, at least, the two were at peace with their lots.

MOSES: View from a Height

There has never been another prophet in Israel like Moses,
whom the LORD knew face to face.

Deuteronomy 34:10 NLT

As his life drew to a close, Moses had lived 120 years: forty years as the son of an Egyptian princess, forty years of a happy homelife with the respect of his father-in-law Jethro, and forty exhausting years of leading the obstinate Israelites through treacherous territory. Now only the Jordan River stood between him and the Promised Land of Canaan.

But he wouldn't cross the Jordan. Because of his disobedience recorded in Numbers 20:1–13, he would see the Promised Land from Mt. Nebo but never enter it. Moses accepted God's decision. In his last speech he blessed his people and told them, "He [God] loves his people; all his holy ones are in his hands," and "There is no one like the God of Israel" (Deuteronomy 33:3, 26 NLT). Moses trusted his life to God and accepted what the future held for him. Contentment filled his heart even when he knew he wouldn't enter the Promised Land.

At times when you review your life, do you remember the happy moments best? Can you accept what God has in store for you? Life does have hills and valleys. When you think about the grace of God, the hard times lose their focus. They fade from memory while the high points still catch sunlight.

JUDAS ISCARIOT: The Betrayer of Jesus

The evening meal was in progress, and the devil had already prompted Judas, the son of Simon Iscariot, to betray Jesus.

John 13:2 NIV

Have you ever wondered what it would have been like to hang out with Jesus? Judas Iscariot was just one of the twelve apostles who had a chance to do that for three years—sharing meals with Him, sitting under His teaching, and asking Him questions. As rich as that experience would have been, how then did he become known as a betrayer of Christ?

The Gospel of John gives us a hint. Judas had an unchecked character flaw that was revealed when he objected to Mary pouring expensive perfume on Jesus' feet and then wiping them with her hair (John 12:3–4). Verse six says he didn't object "because he cared about the poor but because he was a thief; as keeper of the money bag, he used to help himself to what was put into it." If Mary had sold the perfume to give the proceeds to the poor, a portion of it would have ended up in Judas' pocket.

Satan saw Judas' weakness for unlawful financial gain and prompted Judas to betray Jesus—something he did for a mere thirty pieces of silver. What character flaw do you see in your own life that makes you vulnerable to an attack by Satan? What are you doing to overcome it?

AARON: When It's Time to Take a Stand

Moses saw that the people were running wild and that Aaron had let them get out of control and so become a laughingstock to their enemies. So he stood at the entrance to the camp and said, "Whoever is for the LORD, come to me." And all the Levites rallied to him.

Exodus 32:25–26 NIV

Where would Moses and the people of Israel have been without his brother Aaron? He acted as Moses' mouthpiece to Pharaoh in Egypt. He was an instrument in the hand of God as He performed the miracles that convinced Pharaoh to set the Hebrews free from slavery. Later, Aaron had the amazing privilege and responsibility of starting Israel's formal priesthood.

Yet Aaron had his moments of weakness. The best known being his part in Israel's fall into idolatry. Moses had ascended Mount Sinai and stayed there longer than the people had expected, so they pressured Aaron to fashion a golden calf to worship.

Aaron had an opportunity to stand strong for God, but instead he chose to "go along to get along" so he played a key role in the idolatry. The results were tragic. Not only were the people of God involved in pagan revelry, but thousands of them died as a result of their sin.

One of the most important lessons of Aaron's failure to stand up to the demands of the Israelites is this: what we say, what we do, and what we tolerate has consequences.

Do you stand strong for God, even when you know that doing so goes against what is popular? Or do you "keep the peace" by going along with what dishonors Him and brings reproach on His church?

JONATHAN: Complete Surrender

Jonathan said to David,
"Whatever you want me to do, I'll do for you."
1 Samuel 20:4 NIV

Jonathan was a prince, the son of the King of Israel. He had proven himself in battle multiple times, and as the oldest son of Saul, Jonathan was next in line to the throne—that is, until a young man named David came along.

First the prophet Samuel anointed David as the future king of Israel, then David killed the Philistine Goliath, and then he gained fame for successfully leading men in battles. Jonathan had plenty of reasons to be jealous of David, but he wasn't. In fact, 1 Samuel 18:1 (NIV) says, "Jonathan became one in spirit with David, and he loved him as himself."

What devotion to a man who would take Jonathan's birthright! Jonathan's love and faithfulness to David remained steadfast even as his father Saul turned against David. Even as Saul was trying to kill David, Jonathan pledged his fidelity to him.

Ultimately, Jesus would be born from the line of David and become King of kings—ruler over all creation. This King demands our all, but it is the sweetest of demands. When we're faced with this King, what is our response? Do we respond like Jonathan and say, "Whatever you want me to do, I'll do for you"?

THE CENTURION AT THE CROSS:
Too Late—or Just in Time?

Now when the centurion, and they that were with him, watching
Jesus, saw the earthquake, and those things that were done,
they feared greatly, saying, Truly this was the Son of God.

Matthew 27:54 KJV

Scared?

Let me tell you about scared. The centurion didn't just turn up at the conclusion of the crucifixion and proclaim some immortal words. In all likelihood he was in charge of the "soldiers of the governor" who whipped, spat on, and mocked Jesus. He likely gave the orders that drove the nails through His hands and feet.

Then the sky darkened and the earth shook and the realization came to him that he had just "killed" the son of a powerful god! It would have terrified the bravest of men. Hopefully, someone had a quiet word with him afterward. He had recognized Jesus for who He really was. All he had to do was accept Him as his Savior to know peace forever.

We don't know how his life turned out—but he would certainly have been among the ones Jesus asked His Father to forgive (Luke 23:34).

We don't always give our Lord the respect He deserves. Some of us, through the way we live our lives, treat Him pretty shabbily. None of us will have treated Him the way the centurion did, and yet even he was given a second chance.

Don't be scared. Be embraced in the love and forgiveness of the Son of God.

SAMSON: Revenge of the Hairy Judge

Samson judged Israel for twenty years during the period when the Philistines dominated the land.

Judges 15:20 NLT

In the days before the Israelite kings, there were judges. Samson, one in a long line of judges, was tasked with managing disputes, but also with protecting the people. The record of his dedication to protect included a war against the Philistines in which he destroyed a thousand enemies using only the jawbone of a donkey. He destroyed crops by tying the tails of foxes together and sending them through the fields with torches tied between their tails. He physically tore the city gates off their hinges, leaving an enemy city unprotected.

While all that sounds impressive, this judge engaged in almost every act based on his desire for revenge.

He would be deceived by Delilah, his hair would be cut, and his eyes gouged out. It was in his final act that he is remembered for praying. As a blind slave in Philistia, Samson would use his strength to destroy the Philistine temple by pushing down the main pillars and causing the structure to collapse. Even in this final act Samson expressed a desire for revenge for the loss of his eyes.

Samson made enemies easily, but friends seemed harder to come by. His life demonstrated little in the way of forgiveness. God used Samson's violent actions to deliver His people, true, but Samson himself lived his days out angrily seeking revenge.

ISAAC: Wool Over His Eyes

*And Isaac trembled very exceedingly, and said, Who? where is he
that hath taken venison, and brought it me, and I have eaten
of all before thou camest, and have blessed him?*

Genesis 27:33 KJV

Isaac had lived long and, thinking that his end was near—he
was blind and probably in failing health—he told his eldest
son, Esau, to go hunting and make him his favorite stew. He
said he would bless Esau when he brought the wild game
as a meal.

Isaac had no idea that his wife, Rebekah, had overheard
and would trick him and cheat Esau so that Esau's twin,
Jacob, would get the blessing. Rebekah stewed the meat
from a young goat. She then covered Jacob's arms and neck
with hairy goat skin so that when his blind father touched
him he would seem to be Esau. She then sent him to be
blessed.

It worked! Esau lost his blessing while trying—almost
for the first time—to be an obedient son.

Isaac knew very well that he could not distinguish one
son from the other by sight, and could have been more
careful. It seems clear that Isaac and Rebekah's relationship
lacked openness. God worked out His purpose through
Isaac's mistake, but we can hope to be remembered for wiser
behavior.

NATHAN: Conscience of the King

*The LORD sent Nathan the prophet to tell David
this story: "There were two men in a certain town.
One was rich, and one was poor."*
2 Samuel 12:1 NLT

Nathan the prophet had to tell hard truths to David, the popular king of Israel. When David decided to build a temple for the Lord, Nathan had to tell him his son Solomon would build it. As David's life drew to a close, Nathan had to give him the sad news that one of his sons, Adonijah, intended to betray his father and take control of the kingdom. Nathan revealed the plot and convinced David to quickly appoint Solomon as king (1 Kings 1:5–20).

Nathan's greatest challenge occurred when he confronted David over his adultery with Bathsheba and murder of her husband Uriah, one of his faithful soldiers. To reveal David's grievous sin, Nathan told the story of a rich man who believed his powerful position allowed him to steal a lamb from a poor man. David was furious and told Nathan, "This man deserves to die."

"You are that man!" Nathan replied. David was devastated and confessed, "I have sinned against the Lord."

Nathan proved to be a wise, fearless counselor and friend to David. Through the word of God and a good, honorable friend like Nathan who is unafraid to tell the truth, a Christian can see his own shortcomings and overcome them.

LAZARUS: Back from the Grave

*Now a man named Lazarus was sick. He was from Bethany,
the village of Mary and her sister Martha . . . So the sisters
sent word to Jesus, "Lord, the one you love is sick."*

John 11:1, 3 NIV

As you lie on your sickbed, hoping Jesus shows up in time
to heal you, your sisters, Mary and Martha, are doing
everything they know to do to help you—including sending
word to Jesus about your condition. But He doesn't show up
in time and you fade away and die.

The next thing you know, you hear a loud, familiar
voice calling to you, "Lazarus, come out!" (John 11:43).
Resurrection power surges through your body as you open
your eyes to discover that you're wrapped in grave clothes
and are lying in a tomb. You obey your friend's command
and leave the cave to find a stunned crowd. Several people
begin to free you from your grave clothes, and you can
hardly believe what has taken place. You were dead, but now
you're alive.

Jesus performs a similar miracle every time a sinner,
who is dead in sin repents, turning toward Him. He calls us
forth from spiritual death and eternal separation from Him
to everlasting life in a heavenly mansion. As Colossians
2:13 (NIV) says, "When you were dead in your sins and in
the uncircumcision of your flesh, God made you alive with
Christ."

Hallelujah!

What Did That Man's Name Mean?

Just as today, some biblical names had meanings.
Here are a few of those meanings,
including names of some men in this book.

EDOM: Red

ELEAZAR: God is helper

ELI: Lofty

ELIEZER: God of help

ELIJAH: Jehovah is God

ELISHA: God is savior

ENOCH: Initiated

EPHRAIM: Double fruit

ESAU: Rough, hairy

EUTYCHUS: Fortunate

EZEKIEL: God will strengthen

EZRA: Aid

ABRAHAM'S SERVANT:
Selflessness in His Work

Then he prayed, "LORD, God of my master Abraham, make me successful today, and show kindness to my master Abraham."

Genesis 24:12 NIV

Are you comfortable petitioning God and asking Him for success, or does the thought of praying for your own success make you feel a little self-serving?

Well, there is nothing wrong with praying for success. In fact, the Bible encourages us to pray that we be successful in all we do. The key is in what motivates us to pray for success.

There are two main schools of thought today when it comes to praying for success—the first being rooted in the idea that God wants His people to be successful in everything they do. . . personally successful and financially successful.

The second school, which is more rooted in what the written Word of God teaches, holds that when we pray for success, it should be with an eye firmly focused on the purposes of God, His kingdom, and other people.

The latter is how Abraham's eldest servant prayed.

The beginning of this man's prayer demonstrates the kind of selflessness—the kind of "others-centeredness"—God wants to see in all those who serve Him. Yes, he prayed for success, but the kind of success that would benefit another person. That makes this one of the Bible's "model prayers."

So go ahead and selflessly pray with Abraham's servant, "Lord, God. . .make me successful today, and show kindness to _____."

JOSEPH: Breaking the Law

"Because Joseph her husband was faithful to the law, and yet did not want to expose her to public disgrace, he had in mind to divorce her quietly. But after he had considered this, an angel of the Lord appeared to him in a dream and said, "Joseph son of David, do not be afraid to take Mary home as your wife."

Matthew 1:19–20 NIV

For someone who must have played an important role in Jesus' upbringing, we know surprisingly little about Joseph, Jesus' foster father. We know he was a carpenter from Nazareth and he was a man who followed the Law. He also appears to have been an honorable, caring man—someone who followed not just the letter of the Law, but the spirit as well.

When he discovered that his betrothed, Mary, was already pregnant, he had every right under the Law to divorce her quickly and publicly, but that's not what he chose. Joseph sought to quietly divorce her and spare her public disgrace. God's plan, however, didn't include divorce, and He sent His angel to reassure Joseph.

Joseph was faithful to God, even when it meant sacrificing certain "rights" under the Law. Joseph is an example to men even today. When someone wrongs you, do you demand that the Law be fulfilled?

God's Word teaches that the Law is not intended to right the wrongs done to us. Rather the Law is intended to convict us of our sin. Thanks be to God that something much better than the Law came, namely Christ, and satisfied its requirements in order to save us.

DAVID: Lions and Giants and Bears

*David said to Saul, "Let no one lose heart on account of this
Philistine; your servant will go and fight him." Saul replied,
"You are not able to go out against this Philistine and fight
him; you are only a young man, and he has
been a warrior from his youth."*

1 Samuel 17:32–33 NIV

David was the baby of his family. He had been tending
sheep until his father sent him to the battlefield with food
for his brothers.

When he saw that Goliath the giant was taunting
the army of the people of God, David was infuriated and
insisted he be allowed to take him down.

Well, what battle training did this young man have?
Okay, he had killed a bear and a lion in defense of his sheep.
He was handy with a slingshot. But are we supposed to
believe that prepared him for Goliath?

No. What prepared him was his faith. In front of two
armies David declared there was a God in Israel and that
God didn't need swords or spears to save. If David had had
the slightest doubt, he would probably have died in that
encounter. Instead he stepped forward in absolute trust. . .and
won the day!

Do any "giants" need to be brought down in your life?
You don't need a bigger weapon or to be a bigger man. . .you
just need a bigger faith. Remember, Goliath the giant was
small fry to God the Creator!

SILAS: Shining in the Shadows

The crowd joined in the attack against Paul and Silas,
and the magistrates ordered them to be
stripped and beaten with rods.

Acts 16:22 NIV

Silas was a leader, prophet, missionary, prayer warrior, and one of the apostle Paul's most trusted ministry partners. Most of us spend very little time thinking about him. If we read what's actually written about Silas, we gain a great deal of respect for this man who stood faithfully for God and with Paul.

One of the most compelling stories featuring Silas was a story set in prison. He and Paul had been placed there after casting a spirit out of a female slave that pestered them. Her owner thought this made her less valuable, so he had the two men arrested and beaten, accusing them of breaking the law.

At midnight, when most people were sleeping, Paul and Silas were praying and singing. The other prisoners quietly listened. An earthquake, a near suicide by the guard, and a revival service followed this time of worship.

It wouldn't be out of line to suggest that Christians in the first century would have known the personal character of Silas. His name would have evoked memories of the faithfulness and leadership qualities he possessed.

Not every leader shines best in the spotlight. Some will take common tasks and turn them into opportunities for praise to God—who causes all things to work together for good to those who love Him (Romans 8:28).

JACOB: He Knows a Better Way?

The boys grew up, and Esau became a skillful hunter,
a man of the open country, while Jacob was content to stay
at home among the tents. Isaac, who had a taste for
wild game, loved Esau, but Rebekah loved Jacob.

Genesis 25:27-28 NIV

Jacob is a study in the paradox of God's sovereignty and man's responsibility.

God had clearly told Rebekah that she would bear twins and that the firstborn would serve his (slightly) younger brother.

As the verse above shows, the boys' parents played favorites. Jacob's mother almost certainly told him that God's promises to Abraham would come to him. But Jacob wasn't willing to wait and took advantage of Esau's weariness after a hunt and convinced him to trade his birthright for a bowl of stew.

Later, Rebekah and Jacob conspired to get the patriarchal blessing that Isaac had intended for Esau.

These efforts to "help" God keep His promises bring to mind the manipulations of Jacob's grandmother, Sarah. It was becoming a family tradition to run ahead of God.

Jacob, the good son who stayed at home with Mom, learned to be a manipulator and got quite good at it. But people came to distrust him, and he to fear them.

Would God have accomplished His purpose without all that intervention? We know that He could have, and He likely would have, had Jacob only trusted Him to act.

NOAH: No Questions Asked

Noah was a righteous man, the only blameless person living on earth at the time, and he walked in close fellowship with God.

Genesis 6:9 NLT

God gave Noah specific directions for building the ark. "Use cypress wood," God directed, "and waterproof it with tar." He gave the dimensions of the ark, the number of decks, and described locations for the window and the door. Noah did what he was told. No questions asked.

God listed the birds, domestic animals, wild animals, and small animals to be brought inside the boat. He gave the number of each—seven pairs of every animal approved for eating and sacrifice, and one pair of all the others. Noah did everything exactly as God commanded. No questions asked.

When you read the account of Noah in Genesis chapters 6–9, what stands out is the businesslike way that Noah built the ark. Would such clear directions be followed today? Or would the builder ask, "Can I substitute pine for cypress? Would mortar work as well as tar? Why a window there? Wouldn't we need an extra door?"

Noah was not only a hero of faith but also an example of what it means to be an obedient, diligent worker. If you were an employer, wouldn't you jump at the chance to hire a man such as Noah? As an employee, wouldn't you find the door always open if you had the attitude and dedication of Noah?

THE LAME BEGGAR: God-Praiser

And a certain man lame from his mother's womb was carried,
whom they laid daily at the gate of the temple which is called
Beautiful, to ask alms of them that entered into the temple.

Acts 3:2 KJV

You aren't known by your name, but rather, for your physical disability that you've had since birth. Hospitals, long-term care facilities, or disability benefits as we know them today didn't exist, so, as a grown man who is over forty (Acts 4:22), your friends pick you up every morning and drop you off at one of the temple gates to beg for alms.

Day after day, you lie on the ground near the gate, living in perpetual survival mode, never daring to hope for a better life. Then Peter and John come walking by, headed for the temple at the hour of prayer. They hear your cry for money, but Peter offers healing instead. And the healing is instantaneous. How could you do anything but enter the temple with them, as this man did, "walking, and leaping, and praising God" (Acts 3:8–9 KJV)?

Even if we aren't physically disabled, we're all not that different from the condition the lame beggar was in. We're all spiritually lame from birth. Even after believing in Christ, we only grow spiritually as we faithfully seek Christ—day after day, just as the beggar sought his daily sustenance. As you find it, leap and praise God.

BARNABAS: Standing Up for Another

*But Barnabas took him and brought him to the apostles.
He told them how Saul on his journey had seen the Lord
and that the Lord had spoken to him, and how in Damascus
he had preached fearlessly in the name of Jesus.*

Acts 9:27 NIV

After encountering Jesus on the Damascus Road, Saul would become the most famous and influential missionary of all time. However, even though he was a changed man with a new purpose, the Christians of Jerusalem were understandably suspicious, even fearful.

Saul had a well-earned reputation as a man who hated the church—and who had made it his life's goal to stop this new movement we now call Christianity. This he had done by viciously persecuting every Christian who crossed his path.

But Saul had an earthly advocate, a Jewish Christian from Cyprus named Barnabas. While the Jerusalem Christians wanted nothing to do with Saul, Barnabas embraced him as a "new creation" in Jesus Christ and also took a personal interest in mentoring him, knowing that God had called this man to do great things for the kingdom of God.

Barnabas took what, humanly speaking, looked like a big risk by hitching his wagon to Saul. In the same way, we should be on the lookout for new brothers and sisters in Christ—some of them from very rough backgrounds—to stand up for them and mentor them so that they can be all God intends them to be.

JOSEPH: Flee from Temptation

She caught him by his cloak and said, "Come to bed with me!"
But he left his cloak in her hand and ran out of the house.

Genesis 39:12 NIV

Joseph's life is a story of God's providence and rescue of His people. Sold into slavery by his jealous brothers, Joseph found himself a household slave of Potiphar, the captain of Pharaoh's guard. Throughout it all, God was with Joseph. The Bible tells us that Joseph even prospered while he was a slave. God blessed not only Joseph, but He also blessed Potiphar's household because of Joseph.

However, there was danger in Potiphar's house—Potiphar's wife. Genesis 39:6–7 says that Joseph was well-built and handsome, and Potiphar's wife noticed. She tempted Joseph to commit adultery day after day, but Joseph refused. During one such episode, she caught him by his cloak and tried to lure him to bed, but Joseph left his cloak and fled from the temptation.

First Corinthians 6:18 (NIV) explicitly tells us to "flee from sexual immorality." Other verses instruct us to do the same with other temptations: 1 Corinthians 10:14 tells us to flee from idolatry, and 1 Timothy 6:11 says to flee from ungodliness. The Bible is clear that one of the best ways to resist temptation is to remove ourselves from its presence. When faced with temptation, don't let yourself be ensnared. Do like Joseph did—flee!

CLEOPAS: Confused but Still Faithful

And it came to pass, as he sat at meat with them, he took bread, and blessed it, and brake, and gave to them. And their eyes were opened, and they knew him; and he vanished out of their sight.

Luke 24:30–31 KJV

Cleopas (and his unnamed friend) did two things worthy of mention. They were leaving Jerusalem after their leader had been crucified. Perhaps they were avoiding persecution. They had also heard rumors of Jesus rising from the dead, but didn't know what to think.

Then a stranger walked alongside them, explaining that all was as it should be. After a long and troubling day, they planned to sleep that night in a village. The stranger would have walked on, but they invited him to stay, offering food and shelter.

After recognizing Jesus, they proclaimed that He was indeed alive to the other disciples.

To recap: In sharing what they had, they showed love to their neighbor (and, unknowingly, their God) as He had taught them. Then they proclaimed their experience with the risen Lord and how He had affected them.

Guess what happened! When they did these things, Jesus appeared!

Being confused about faith isn't an unusual thing. Cleopas was certainly confused, but he lived his faith nevertheless and had it confirmed in the most wonderful way. If you still have questions, try living the life for a while; walk the walk a few miles (John 7:17). You might be amazed by who you meet on the journey.

What Did That Man's Name Mean?

Just as today, some biblical names had meanings.
Here are a few of those meanings,
including names of some men in this book.

FELIX: Happy

FESTUS: Festal

GAD: Good fortune

GAMALIEL: Reward of God

GAZZAM: Devourer

GEMALLI: Camel driver

GIDDALTI: I have made great

GIDEON: Warrior

GILEAD: Heap of testimony

GINNETHON: Gardener

GOLIATH: Exile

GUNI: Protected

SOLOMON: A Hope and a Future

King Solomon will be blessed, and David's throne will remain secure before the LORD forever.

1 Kings 2:45 NIV

He was the son of the most famous king in Israel. He would succeed his father on the throne, but his pedigree wasn't without controversy. Both of his parents, David and Bathsheba, had committed adultery at the beginning of their relationship, which led to murder in an unsuccessful attempt to cover up this indiscretion.

Despite the sins of his parents, Solomon was judged faithful based on his own relationship with God.

Solomon was not the oldest of King David's sons nor was he the most cunning. In fact, there was a plot to place one of his half brothers, Adonijah, on the throne without King David's consent. The king was made aware of the plot and put an end to it quickly.

Solomon stood before his father, David, and received both instruction and blessing. David also supplied Solomon with materials he would need to construct a temple. When King David died, Solomon knew he didn't possess the experience to lead his people, but he did possess the desire to lead well.

We sometimes believe that we're doomed to behave just like our parents. But we should be encouraged when reading Solomon's story because we see that God's grace allows people to be used despite their past and in spite of any shortcomings of their parents. The cycle of sin can be broken.

GIDEON: Timid Audacity

Then Gideon said to God, "Do not be angry with me...
allow me one more test with the fleece."

Judges 6:39 NIV

When the invading Midianites and the Amalekites camped in the Valley of Jezreel, the Spirit of God came over Gideon, and he gathered an army of Israelites to defeat them. But he still asked God to prove His support.

Gideon asked God to make the dew of the night fall on a fleece and not on the threshing floor. When morning showed that God had obliged, Gideon apologetically asked God to repeat the performance, but with a dry fleece and a dewy threshing floor. God graciously complied.

God pared Gideon's troops from thirty-two thousand to three hundred and let Gideon eavesdrop on the enemy, revealing that God had prepared them to expect defeat.

Gideon ordered his men into three companies. They surrounded the enemy camp, and at his signal, blew their trumpets, broke the pitchers that hid their lamps, and shouted, "For the LORD and for Gideon!"

The enemy warriors began attacking each other and fleeing. Gideon sent word to his countrymen, who pursued the Midianites and Amalekites, ending their oppression.

Gideon is regularly ridiculed for asking God to prove Himself. On the other hand, lots of people seeking God's will say they are "putting out a fleece." Also through history, God gave many signs to validate His works. Among the clearest was that shepherds would find a babe wrapped in swaddling clothes, lying in a manger.

NATHANAEL: Double Take

Then Nathanael exclaimed,
"Rabbi, you are the Son of God—the King of Israel!"
John 1:49 NLT

How would you react if a person could tell you what you were doing and even thinking before they met you? When meeting Jesus for the first time, Nathanael changed from asking, "Can anything good come from Nazareth?" to "You are the Son of God!" (John 1:46, 49 NLT). The sudden reversal happened because Jesus told Nathanael he was "a genuine son of Israel—a man of complete integrity" (v. 47 NLT). Jesus then described angels descending on the Son of Man.

Now, whereas Nathanael was "a man of complete integrity," Jacob (Israel) lacked integrity. He had deceived his father for his brother Esau's blessing. However, in Genesis 28:12, Jacob was blessed with seeing angels descending from heaven. Could Nathanael have been thinking about the paradox of Jacob, and Jesus referred to what was on his mind?

Whatever Nathanael was thinking about, his mind was on scripture because he recognized Jesus as the one that Moses and the prophets wrote about. Nathanael became a steadfast disciple. He began following Jesus in the first chapter of John, and was present in the last chapter after the resurrection of Jesus.

Nathanael doesn't occupy a large section of the Bible—he is mentioned only six times—but this encounter reveals how knowledge of the Word of God can change a questioning mind into a believing mind.

JOSEPH: God Works in Mysterious Ways

"Joseph is still alive! In fact, he is ruler of all Egypt."
Genesis 45:26 NIV

One can't help but wonder at the life of Joseph, the favored son of Jacob and firstborn son of Rachel. God led Joseph through a roller coaster of ups and downs which were instrumental in the creation of the nation of Israel. From his status as privileged son, Joseph was sold into slavery by jealous brothers. But God led Joseph to become the servant of an Egyptian official and brought him prosperity.

Then a false accusation landed Joseph in prison. Still, God was with Joseph. God inspired Joseph to interpret Pharaoh's dream, and he was raised to the second highest position in Egypt. God used Joseph there not only to prepare Egypt for upcoming years of famine, but also to provide a place for nascent Israel to prosper and grow into a nation.

Joseph's rise to greatness seemed unlikely at many periods of his life, yet God was at work, guiding events in order to provide not only for Joseph, but for God's people at large.

When you're going through rough times, don't despair. Remember that "neither death nor life, neither angels nor demons, neither the present nor the future, nor any powers, neither height nor depth, nor anything else in all creation, will be able to separate us from the love of God that is in Christ Jesus our Lord" (Romans 8:38–39 NIV).

BARZILLAI: A Faithful Friend. . . in Spite of Popular Opinion

*Now Barzillai was very old, eighty years of age. He had provided
for the king during his stay in Mahanaim,
for he was a very wealthy man.*

2 Samuel 19:32 NIV

Barzillai is not one of the better-known men of Old
Testament times, but the biblical account of his life and his
relationship with King David can teach us something about
standing strong for a friend—or what God has taught us is
right—even when there is risk involved.

David's son, Absalom, had turned public opinion
against him, to the point where the king had to literally run
for his life. And while the Bible doesn't tell us that Barzillai
knew David personally, he definitely knew about David and
understood that he was a leader who was truly a man after
God's own heart.

The Bible recounts Barzillai as a man who extended
kindness and support to someone in desperate need—and
probably at great personal risk. Though his decision to
support David wouldn't have fared well in public opinion
polls of the time, he never hesitated in standing up for God's
anointed leader of the nation of Israel.

We live in a time when identifying ourselves with Jesus
Christ isn't as popular and accepted as it once was—now
standing for God's principles opens us up to scorn and
rejection. But God calls us to be modern-day Barzillais,
people who will stand up for Him even though doing so
presents risks.

MATTHEW: Tax Collector Turned Evangelist

As Jesus went on from there, he saw a man named Matthew sitting at the tax collector's booth. "Follow me," he told him, and Matthew got up and followed him.

Matthew 9:9 NIV

Today we know Matthew as the one of the four beloved writers whom God used to chronicle the life of Jesus so we would have it, could refer to it, and could be transformed by it. But Matthew wouldn't have felt the love during his era. He was from Galilee, and while Rome occupied the area, collaborators like Matthew were the ones who collected taxes for them. Tax collectors were also known to become rich by charging more than was due.

Along came Jesus, who saw Matthew sitting at the tax collector's booth and issued a simple command: "Follow me"—and Matthew instantly left his life of luxury for an unknown adventure. Matthew invited Jesus and His disciples back to his house, which was probably a large residence, where they dined with other tax collectors and sinners, because he wanted them to have access to Jesus. And Jesus gladly ate with them.

Sometimes the most religious among us question our willingness to hang out with people who aren't living up to our standards, just like the Pharisees did Jesus in this circumstance. Do it anyway. As Jesus answered the Pharisees, "It is not the healthy who need a doctor, but the sick."

ELIJAH: Baal's Worst Nightmare

And it came to pass, when Ahab saw Elijah, that Ahab said unto him, Art thou he that troubleth Israel? And he answered, I have not troubled Israel; but thou, and thy father's house, in that ye have forsaken the commandments of the LORD, and thou hast followed Baalim.

1 Kings 18:17–18 KJV

Elijah strides onto the biblical stage fully formed and impressive. All we know about him is that his name means "Yahweh is my God," and he isn't happy!

Israel has had a series of kings, culminating in Ahab, who have relied less and less on God and allowed the worshippers of pagan gods to have more and more influence. Primary among these are the worshippers of Baal.

When Elijah declares that enough is enough, he says God will send a drought on the disobedient kingdom. There will be no rain, or even dew, for three years. Who is supposed to be the god of rain and dew? Baal.

Elijah is no less direct when he challenges the priests of Baal to a show of divine power before witnesses. Baal fails to burn an offering of meat, but the Lord sends down heavenly fire to incinerate two soaked bullock carcasses.

Elijah wasn't all bravado, though. When God told him to hide, he hid. When God sent birds with food, he laid low and survived.

Then, just as he appeared, he disappeared! Elijah's life raises the question, what can't a man do with the power of God behind him?

TIMOTHY: The Promise of Youth

Timothy, guard what God has entrusted to you.
Avoid godless, foolish discussions with those who
oppose you with their so-called knowledge.

1 Timothy 6:20 NLT

Paul, a broken, misunderstood apostle, found a young missionary partner who was not fully Jewish and suffered from an unknown stomach ailment. Mutual misfits? Yes, but God uses foolish things to confound those who think they know it all (1 Corinthians 1:27).

Timothy was a spiritual son to Paul and was taken on many missionary journeys. He proved himself worthy time after time. In fact, Paul told Timothy to refuse to be disheartened when others sought to equate his ability with his age. Timothy was to provide leadership and set an example that even older Christians could follow.

The books of 1 and 2 Timothy are filled with a mentor's advice to a trainee. Paul set the bar high for Timothy, and with great expectations came a great outcome. Paul expected more, and Timothy delivered.

When it came to Timothy's life, we see an incredible investment on the part of his mentor, Paul. Like a parent seeking to train his child, Paul used time, instruction, and example to create an atmosphere of growth for this young man. This example can provide a blueprint for interactions with our own children and those whom God may call us to mentor.

ISAIAH: Getting the Call

*Also I heard the voice of the Lord, saying, Whom shall I send,
and who will go for us? Then said I, Here am I; send me.*

Isaiah 6:8 KJV

If we knew the extent of things we have to do, sometimes we might be less eager to agree to do them.

Isaiah spent more than sixty years delivering God's messages to Judah describing human activity to the last age of the earth. He spoke for God during the reign of four kings of Judah. Often he was received as Jesus noted: "A prophet has no honor in his own country" (John 4:44 NIV).

In fact, the message God gave him bore this out: "And he said, Go, and tell this people, Hear ye indeed, but understand not; and see ye indeed, but perceive not" (Isaiah 6:9 KJV).

Maybe the people of Judah paid little attention to Isaiah because much of what he foretold was not scheduled to happen soon, or even in their lifetimes. We have been told by astronomers that the sun will burn out someday, but we give it no thought because they tell us it won't happen anytime soon.

It's the same with God. We can get the impression that His delays mean He won't do a thing. That's not the case. "The Lord is not slow in keeping his promise. . .instead he is patient with you, not wanting anyone to perish" (2 Peter 3:9 NIV).

PAUL: Name Change

When I was with the Jews, I lived like a Jew to bring the Jews to Christ. . . . When I am with the Gentiles who do not follow the Jewish law, I too live apart from that law so I can bring them to Christ. But I do not ignore the law of God; I obey the law of Christ.

1 Corinthians 9:20–21 NLT

When Paul first appeared in the Gospel record, he was Saul of Tarsus, a zealous Jew who tried to stamp out the Christian faith. Following a heart-to-heart talk with Jesus on the road to Damascus, Saul was baptized. After his conversion the apostles in Jerusalem accepted him, but some Christians looked upon him with suspicion. He eventually went to Tarsus. Later, Barnabas went there and rescued Saul from obscurity, and the Holy Spirit sent them on a missionary journey.

On the island of Cyprus Saul made his first recorded Gentile convert, Sergius Paulus, the Roman governor. After this success, Saul became known as Paul, derived from the Latin family name, Paulus. Apparently the name change was Paul's desire to embrace his role as an apostle to the Gentiles (Acts 13:7–9, 13).

With the new birth and baptism a person leaves behind a life of hate, rage, and sin to embrace a better life. We can also make the lives of others better by presenting Christ to them using culturally relevant methods.

What Did That Man's Name Mean?

Just as today, some biblical names had meanings.
Here are a few of those meanings,
including names of some men in this book.

HABAKKUK: Embrace

HAGGAI: Festive

HAM: Hot

HANANIAH: God has favored

HANOCH: Initiated, favor of God

HELAH: Rust

HEN: Grace

HEROD: Heroic

HEZEKIAH: Strengthened of God

HILKIAH: Portion of God

HURI: Linen worker

HUSHAI: Hasty

MEPHIBOSHETH: The Well-Treated "Dead Dog"

Mephibosheth bowed down and said, "What is your servant, that you should notice a dead dog like me?"

2 Samuel 9:8 NIV

Mephibosheth, who had crippled feet, saw himself as a "dead dog"—unworthy of being noticed by anybody, let alone King David. But David didn't see him that way, especially since he was the son of his best friend, Jonathan. So David sought to show him kindness, even going so far as to restore the land that belonged to his grandfather, Saul, and inviting him to eat at the king's table.

Wild dogs ran amok in the east at the time of Mephibosheth's reference and people often showed contempt for them—a reaction he would have been accustomed to, given his physical condition. And then, out of nowhere, David offered him mercy beyond imagination. David's action is similar to Christ's mercy on us.

Do you remember how you felt the moment the Holy Spirit revealed that you were a sinner in the sight of God, with no hope for eternity apart from Him? You felt the weight of your condition for the first time, then a moment later, recognized that Jesus had paid the price in full to remove your burden and redeem your soul.

Yes, we are redeemed Mephibosheths. As such, we are invited to dine at the marriage supper of the Lamb (Revelation 19:6–9).

BENJAMIN: An Object of Envy?

When portions were served to them from Joseph's table,
Benjamin's portion was five times as much as anyone else's.
So they feasted and drank freely with him.

Genesis 43:34 NIV

The Bible has a lot to say about envy and jealousy, which can be defined as wanting something another person has so badly that we engage in sinful thoughts and actions toward the person who has what we desire.

Envy had moved Joseph's older brothers to sell him into slavery (Genesis 37:18–36). Joseph was clearly their father Jacob's favorite son, and they hated him for it. Only the intervention of Reuben saved Joseph from being murdered by his other brothers.

Many years later, due to a severe famine in Canaan, Joseph and his brothers were reunited in Egypt. At first, the brothers didn't even recognize Joseph, though he knew who they were and put them to the test by treating his youngest brother, Benjamin, with obvious favoritism.

Joseph and Benjamin's ten brothers passed the test set before them. Where before they had acted against Joseph because of the favoritism their father showed him, now they bore no ill-will toward Benjamin because Joseph had treated him with such favor. In fact, they celebrated with him (Genesis 43:34).

The question this story poses to us today is this: when God blesses someone richly—maybe beyond what we might believe they deserve—will we respond to such blessings with jealousy and envy, or will we celebrate from the heart what God has done for another of His children?

THE EUNUCH: Jesus Solves the Mystery

And the eunuch answered Philip, and said, I pray thee, of whom speaketh the prophet this? of himself, or of some other man? Then Philip opened his mouth, and began at the same scripture, and preached unto him Jesus.

Acts 8:34–35 KJV

The Ethiopian eunuch didn't need spectacles, he needed a new perspective. And God positioned Philip perfectly to provide it.

A high official of the queen in Ethiopia, he had traveled to Jerusalem to worship God. Philip saw him reading scripture in his chariot, like a modern passenger might read the Bible in his car or on the train.

In modern times we know that Christ was referred to many times in the Old Testament (in Isaiah 53, for example), but to many people the figure referred to in these passages was a mystery. The eunuch was obviously confused by what he read. So, Philip, with his firsthand knowledge, took the old words and gave them new life. He told the eunuch that the suffering Savior referred to centuries ago had fulfilled these prophecies.

All those confusing verses now made sense! Jesus was the missing piece in the puzzle. The eunuch looked around, saw some water, and asked to be baptized. God alone knows how this powerful, educated man spread the word when he arrived back home, but He had used Philip powerfully to do his part.

The Old Testament reads quite differently when we view it through the lens of Jesus. So do our lives. So does the world.

URIAH THE HITTITE:
An Unraveled Murder

*"Then the archers shot arrows at your servants from the wall,
and some of the king's men died. Moreover,
your servant Uriah the Hittite is dead."*

2 Samuel 11:24 NIV

It's a bit strange to look at the life of someone by talking about their death, but Uriah the Hittite died in battle serving his country in the army of King David. If this was all we knew then we might have been left thinking that Uriah died honorably in battle. But there's a back story, and Uriah's death was murder. The perpetrator? King David.

While Uriah and Israel's soldiers were at war, David spotted Uriah's wife, Bathsheba, from his window. He started his slide to murder by lusting after the woman, asking about her, inviting her to the palace, sleeping with her, and then discovering she was pregnant with his child.

To cover up his sin, he first brought Uriah from the front lines and encouraged him to go home. If Uriah slept with his wife he could be deceived into believing he was the child's father. When Uriah's sense of duty prevented him from going home, David enacted Plan B. Uriah was placed at the front of the line in war, and when the combat was hottest, he was left to fight alone and die.

Uriah had been one of the elite soldiers in David's army, but his military value was not strong enough to stop the king from killing him to take his wife.

JOB: Why Me, God?

There was a man in the land of Uz, whose name was Job;
and that man was perfect and upright,
and one that feared God, and eschewed evil.

Job 1:1 KJV

Woe upon woe. Job loses his herds, his children, and his health—all in a matter of weeks.

Job was a wealthy man in a time when wealth was measured by the number of sheep, goats, camels, and oxen a man owned. So he lost a fortune and a family and soon after, became sick. He couldn't even say, "At least I still have my health."

We try to understand Job's misery, just as he tried to understand the reason these things happened—assuming there was a reason.

Several of Job's friends came to him offering reasons. How wonderful that they had the answer when Job, knowing his own life so well, could think of none!

It would be easy for us to think God allowed an eternally horrible thing to happen to Job's family. But we are given no reason to think that Job's children were not also God's children. Job doesn't speak of that possibility as another part of his calamities.

But the events show a frightening aspect of God's character. It tends to make us remember that the Bible often tells us to fear God. That's neither warm nor fuzzy, is it? God has purposes that don't always align with ours. The best we can do in those cases is to submit to His will.

PAUL: Singing at Midnight

Don't worry about anything; instead, pray about everything.
Tell God what you need, and thank him for all he has done.
Philippians 4:6 NLT

On his second missionary journey, Paul traveled with Silas. In Philippi, Paul delivered a slave girl from a fortune-telling spirit. She'd earned a lot of money for her owners, so they stirred up a mob. The city officials (not knowing Paul and Silas were Roman citizens) illegally ordered them stripped, beaten, and thrown into prison.

That night Paul and Silas were singing and praying. What kind of songs were they singing? They undoubtedly were songs of praise to God. Suddenly an earthquake opened their chains and cell doors, but Paul assured the alarmed jailer they hadn't escaped. The jailer treated their injuries and fed them, and the next day the city officials released Paul and Silas with an apology.

Events at Philippi had turned into a triumph for Paul. He'd preached to a group of women who were holding a prayer service. He'd baptized a businesswoman and her household. A jailer and his family had been saved. His efforts resulted in a church at Philippi.

Later, while being held for trial in Rome, Paul wrote a letter to the Philippians and said that his chains actually served to advance the gospel (Philippians 1:12). What a positive attitude! Paul looked upon a hardship as another way to show that God was working in his life—an example we can follow today.

LYSIAS: A Lover of Justice

[Paul] also hath gone about to profane the temple: whom we took, and would have judged according to our law. But the chief captain Lysias came upon us, and with great violence took him away out of our hands.

Acts 24:6–7 KJV

Lysias, who was Greek by birth, purchased his Roman citizenship (Acts 22:28), at which time, it is believed, he picked up the forename Claudius. His role as a commander in the Roman army probably put him in charge of over a thousand men.

Paul, on the other hand, was a Roman citizen by birth. As such, he had the full rights of citizenship, including the right to a Roman trial. When Paul ran afoul of the Jewish leaders in Jerusalem, they falsely accused him of being a troublemaker who stirred up rebellions against his own government as well as defiling the temple.

Once Lysias sorted out the details, however, especially after learning that Paul was a Roman citizen, he and his men removed Paul by force so he could get a fair trial.

Lysias stepped into a difficult situation, against the will of the people, to do the right thing even though it was difficult and required force. That's what genuine leadership looks like. Is there a situation in your life that may require a similar response, even if it just requires you to take a forceful stand?

BARTIMAEUS: Lessons in Persistence

Many rebuked him and told him to be quiet, but he shouted all the more, "Son of David, have mercy on me!"

Mark 10:48 NIV

The account of blind Bartimaeus, which is recorded in Mark 10:46–52, is one of those biblical stories with more than one important message—one for Jesus' followers and one for those who actively seek Him.

Bartimaeus made a bit of a scene that day in Jericho as he persistently and loudly called out to Jesus. Jesus' followers that day—being imperfect people following their perfect Lord—had no patience or time for Bartimaeus. To them, he was simply a blind beggar, a societal throw-away to be ignored. Not so with Jesus, who saw not just the man's circumstances but a heart that believed the Savior had something he needed and wanted.

Bartimaeus wasn't about to be shamed into holding his tongue when those around him made it abundantly clear that they didn't want him bothering their Lord. And because of his persistence, he received his sight. . .and a new purpose in life: following Jesus.

The story of blind Bartimaeus stands as an example of transformation through Jesus Christ and as an example of why we should never let others discourage us from calling out to Him. But let's not miss another important lesson in this story: we should always be careful to make certain that our words, attitudes, and actions welcome people to call out to Jesus, not prevent them from doing so.

ELISHA: The Student Succeeds the Teacher

Elisha then picked up Elijah's cloak that had fallen from him and went back and stood on the bank of the Jordan. He took the cloak. . .and struck the water with it. "Where now is the LORD, the God of Elijah?" he asked. When he struck the water, it divided to the right and to the left, and he crossed over.

2 Kings 2:13–14 NIV

Elisha was plowing his field when Elijah called. Knowing this was God's will, Elisha didn't hesitate. Well. . .he did a little. He hesitated long enough to kiss his parents, break apart his plow, cook his oxen, and give the meat to the people. He very definitely wasn't going back to the farming life!

We don't hear anything more about Elisha for several years, implying that he kept his head down, watched, learned, and served. He was a dedicated servant of the prophet of God. Even when he heard the Lord was about to take his master, he refused to leave him.

His reward was a double portion of Elijah's spirit, becoming his recognized successor and performing twice as many miracles. In a foreshadowing of Jesus' miracle of the loaves and the fishes, Elisha fed one hundred men with twenty loaves and even had leftovers.

Spiritual teachers like Elijah are scarce. But if you find one who is a true man of God, then do what Elisha did: watch, learn, and follow.

STEPHEN: A Life Lost and Won

Stephen, a man full of God's grace and power,
performed amazing miracles and signs among the people.
Acts 6:8 NLT

Sometimes, people become leaders because they step forward when others step back. For Moses that man was Joshua, for David that was Solomon, and for the early church that included Stephen.

It was a time of growth for Christians, but there were practical, physical jobs to be done as well—such as distributing food and funds. So the apostles reviewed résumés, talked with human resources, and came up with seven names. And Stephen was one of the men chosen to help.

Stephen was also a gifted speaker and one day was challenged to a debate. The Bible indicates that Stephen won, but the men who lost apparently never earned a good sportsmanship badge. They spread lies that Stephen had blasphemed God. When the lie was believed, Stephen was taken before the high priest where he gave a brilliant defense. His speech, however, was critical of those who refused to see the truth about Jesus and their role in His murder.

The Jewish leaders were furious and had Stephen dragged out of the city and stoned. In spite of the death he faced, Stephen's final words were, "Lord, don't charge them with this sin!"

Watching from the sidelines was a young man who held the coats of those throwing stones. This young man agreed with killing Stephen, but would soon believe as Stephen had. We know the coat holder now as the apostle Paul.

What Did That Man's Name Mean?

Just as today, some biblical names had meanings.
Here are a few of those meanings,
including names of some men in this book.

IBHAR: Choice

IBNEIAH: Built of God

IBZAN: Splendid

ICHABOD: There is no glory

IDBASH: Honeyed

IGEAL: Avenger

ISAAC: Laughter

ISAIAH: God has saved

ISCARIOT: Inhabitant of Kerioth

ISHBI-BENOB: His dwelling is in Nob

ISHMAEL: God will hear

ISRAEL: Ruling with God

JAMES, SON OF ALPHAEUS:
Less Said the Better?

There were also women looking on afar off: among whom
was Mary Magdalene, and Mary the mother of
James the less and of Joses, and Salome.

Mark 15:40 KJV

The disciple "James the less" is mentioned only eight times in the New Testament. Four of those times his name is in a list of the twelve apostles of Jesus. Another four times, he's mentioned in connection with his family.

Nothing is recorded about what he did, said, thought, or wrote.

He was a son of Alphaeus. Levi (Matthew) also had an Alphaeus as his father, and it's possible that they were brothers, but we're not told that. Other name coincidences suggest that the mother of this James may have been a sister-in-law of Jesus' mother, Mary.

None of these possibilities gives even a hint to any events in James's life. But who could deny that God greatly favored this man in calling him to learn under Jesus' teaching? No doubt he taught others what he learned while going about a quiet life. While God has called all believers to proclaim the good news that Jesus, the Son of God, paid the debt of our sins, we're not all called to be pastors, evangelists, or missionaries. He has told most of us to tell that good news as we go about our daily living.

PETER: First to Fight

*Then Simon Peter drew a sword and slashed off the
right ear of Malchus, the high priest's slave.*

John 18:10 NLT

Peter had great faith, but he sometimes got ahead of that
faith, such as when he stepped from the boat to walk on
storm-tossed water to Jesus. On another occasion, Peter was
at the transfiguration of Jesus. He and James and John saw
Moses and Elijah talking with Jesus. Peter, not knowing
what to say, suggested building three shelters to honor them,
but God then put things in proper focus, saying, "This is my
Son, my Chosen One. Listen to him" (Luke 9:35 NLT).

On the night of Jesus' arrest, Peter also acted by reflex.
After the Last Supper, Jesus and the apostles walked to
Gethsemane. Judas the betrayer arrived with the large crowd
to arrest Jesus. Peter was carrying a sword and used it. He
severed Malchus's right ear, although Jesus restored it. Peter
himself needed to be restored, too, after denying Jesus three
times.

Peter eventually saw the benefit of composed endurance
in the face of adversity. Possibly he remembered his own
actions in the garden when he included self-control in
the list of Christian qualities along with faith, goodness,
knowledge, patience, godliness, and love.

A Christian life is a balanced life, one filled with
boldness coupled with self-control, determination balanced
with patience, knowledge overlaid with love, and emotion
tempered with reason (2 Peter 1:5–7).

MELCHIZEDEK: A Type of Christ

Then Melchizedek king of Salem brought out bread and wine.
He was priest of God Most High, and he blessed Abram.

Genesis 14:18-19 NIV

As a king who reigned in Salem (Jerusalem) and was also a priest of God Most High, Melchizedek was quite a rarity. In fact, scripture says he was "without father or mother, without genealogy, without beginning of days or end of life, resembling the Son of God, he remains a priest forever" (Hebrews 7:3 NIV).

Melchizedek was not from the line of Levi (God's chosen tribe for the priesthood), and neither was Jesus. Why does that matter? Consider the question the writer of Hebrews asks (7:11): "If perfection could have been attained through the Levitical priesthood—and indeed the law given to the people established that priesthood—why was there still need for another priest to come, one in the order of Melchizedek, not in the order of Aaron?"

Indeed, Melchizedek was a type of Christ, fore-shadowing (some even believe he was a theophany—a visible manifestation of Christ) the One True Lamb whose eventual sacrifice on the cross as the ultimate High Priest would take away the sin of the world. As such, Melchizedek's actions pointed toward Christ. And Jesus became our high priest in the order of Melchizedek.

ADAM: A Lesson in Keeping Focus

When the woman saw that the fruit of the tree was good for food and pleasing to the eye, and also desirable for gaining wisdom, she took some and ate it. She also gave some to her husband, who was with her, and he ate it.

Genesis 3:6 NIV

In human history, no decision has had such a profound impact on all of humankind as Adam and Eve's decision to disobey God and do the one thing He had barred them from doing. Their decision to eat the fruit from the tree of knowledge of good and evil has affected every human being who has lived since then.

There are many important lessons to learn from Adam and Eve's actions and what they have meant to humans, and one of them is the importance of what we focus on—namely, the goodness of God.

Adam and Eve listened to the devil in snake's clothing and at the same time lost focus on all God had given them and on their fellowship with Him. Consequently, they chose something they believed was better than what they already had.

The apostle Peter warned us, "Be alert and of sober mind. Your enemy the devil prowls around like a roaring lion looking for someone to devour" (1 Peter 5:8 NIV). The devil knows us—he knows our weaknesses and which buttons he can push to divert our attention from the goodness of God.

But we can pluck the fangs out of this lyin' lion by keeping our focus on who God is and what He has done for us.

DAVID: Being the Better Man

He said to his men, "The LORD forbid that I should do such
a thing to my master, the LORD's anointed, or lay my
hand on him; for he is the anointed of the LORD."

1 Samuel 24:6 NIV

David was a faithful servant to an undeserving king. Why? Because he believed Saul had God's backing and David's first loyalty was to God. If the king threw spears at him, then David would have to duck. If Saul planned to kill David, there must be a reason God hadn't explained yet. David didn't approve of Saul's behavior, but he wouldn't go against his rightful king even to save his own life.

Was he a fool? Yes. By worldly standards. He could have claimed the crown and probably done his people a favor. He would have seemed perfectly justified. But he would have been forced to compromise his own standards to do it. In other words, to give his nation a better king he would have had to become a worse man.

Instead, he suffered the taunts and threats and waited for God's plan to play out. Eventually, Saul died and the Lord gave Judah a king with impeccable standards, David, a king who wouldn't let himself or God down—for a while anyway.

As children of the King of kings we should ask how a king or queen ought to behave. . .then live up to those standards, no matter what the world thinks.

THOMAS: Most Likely to be Negative

Then Thomas (also known as Didymus) said to the rest of the disciples, "Let us also go, that we may die with him."

John 11:16 NIV

Thomas was a "glass is half empty" disciple with a side order of trust issues. Maybe, like Thomas, you refuse to believe anything unless you see it with your own eyes.

We really only have three examples of his gloomy spirit. Then again, there are only four total references to things Thomas actually said. The first is when Jesus told His disciples He was going to see Lazarus who had recently died. Thomas assumed the likely outcome would be death for all of them. The second incident was when Jesus said the disciples should know where He was going—heaven—but to paraphrase Thomas, "Nope, don't have a clue."

The third incident is the most notable. After Jesus rose from the dead, Thomas was told that the disciples had seen Him. Thomas said, "Unless I see the nail marks in his hands and put my finger where the nails were, and put my hand into his side, I will not believe" (John 20:25 NIV).

The final thing we read from Thomas indicates a profound change of heart. When he finally saw Jesus following the resurrection, Jesus granted his request. Thomas was overwhelmed and convinced and exclaimed, "My Lord and my God!" (verse 28).

Jesus has always had the power to overcome tough trust issues. For Thomas—for you.

JABEZ: One Man's Prayer

*Jabez cried out to the God of Israel, "Oh, that You would bless
me and enlarge my territory! Let your hand be with me,
and keep me from harm so that I will be free
from pain." And God granted his request.*

1 Chronicles 4:10 NIV

Renowned preacher Charles Spurgeon presented a sermon of
more than 6,800 words, using the 50 words of Jabez's prayer
in 1 Chronicles as a center on which to spread his own.

A recent book's sales pitch says that those who commit
to offering the prayer of Jabez regularly will encounter
God's lavish blessings, and be used by Him to demonstrate
miracle-working power on a daily basis.

But God hasn't said that. In fact, He hasn't told us to
repeat verbatim any of the prayers recorded in the Bible.

Why did the chronicler put the anecdote about Jabez in
the genealogical list? To edify us, of course. Any connection
Jabez may have to the others listed is not told us—only
that he was more honorable than his brothers. While God
certainly does promise to bless us and supply all our needs,
some caution must be exercised: we're not meant to use the
prayer of Jabez like some kind of mantra.

We do know that God commands us to bring our own
needs before Him, though that might or might not include
an enlargement of our borders.

NEBUCHADNEZZAR: King of Beasts

*"I want you all to know about the miraculous signs
and wonders the Most High God has performed for me."*

Daniel 4:2 NLT

The Bible has several incidents showing the dangers of pride. One of the most unusual concerns Nebuchadnezzar, the powerful ruler of Babylon. He had a disturbing dream of a large tree cut down with only the stump and roots remaining. He called for Daniel, a young noble of Judah, to interpret the dream.

Daniel said that the tree's large size, abundant fruit, and shelter to animals represented Nebuchadnezzar and his providing for his subjects. But the tree being cut down showed the king would be driven away and isolated from other people, although the kingdom would be restored because the roots and stump remained. Daniel urged the king to repent of his sins.

Twelve months later, as Nebuchadnezzar walked on the roof of his palace he boasted about his mighty power and the great city, which in his mind he thought he had built with his own hands. Immediately, he became as a beast of the field, eating grass, with his hair matted like feathers, and his nails growing long like claws.

After a time, his sanity returned and Nebuchadnezzar was restored to his throne. In a remarkable letter to his subjects recorded in Daniel chapter four, the king told about all the events that had befallen him and acknowledged that God can humble those who walk in pride.

LOT: The Lingerer

*And while he lingered, the men laid hold upon his hand,
and upon the hand of his wife, and upon the hand of his
two daughters; the LORD being merciful unto him:
and they brought him forth, and set him without the city.*

Genesis 19:16 KJV

Bible commentators aren't sure why Lot lingered after the angels told him to flee Sodom because they were going to destroy it. Some believe he was hesitant because of the property he would lose. Some believe he was waiting to see if his two sons-in-law would leave the city (v. 14). And some believe he grieved for everyone inside. Maybe it was a combination of all three.

In spite of his lingering, the angels showed mercy to Lot, his wife, and their two adult daughters, grabbing them by the hand and leading them out of the city. Lot was undeserving of this mercy. In fact, our modern culture would probably say, "Lot was no angel," given that he offered his two daughters to a mob, and then, once safely tucked away in a cave with his daughters, he got drunk and fell prey to their advances.

But redemption isn't about acting like an angel; instead, it's a power that transforms people who once had no regard for their sin into redeemed sinners who spend their entire lives putting the old sin nature to death. And even though the journey is difficult, they do so with an everlasting joy.

We don't know if Lot did this, but we're certainly called to live that way.

ANDREW: Bringing People to Jesus

Andrew, Simon Peter's brother, was one of the two who heard what John had said and who had followed Jesus. The first thing Andrew did was to find his brother Simon and tell him, "We have found the Messiah."

John 1:40-41 NIV

When we spend time with Jesus, it's only natural that we want to do whatever we can to bring others to Him so they can spend time with Him, too.

Andrew, who would become one of Jesus' twelve apostles, had been a follower of John the Baptist. But after he heard John proclaim that Jesus was "the lamb of God" and then had spent the day with Him, he could barely contain his excitement. He went to find his brother Simon (whom Jesus later renamed "Peter") so he could bring him to meet Jesus.

The Gospel of John reports that it wasn't the last time he brought people to meet the Lord. On the shore of the Sea of Galilee, Andrew brought a boy who had two fish and five barley loaves to Jesus, who then performed a tremendous miracle with that small amount of food (John 6:8–13). And in Jerusalem, he and Philip brought some curious Greeks to meet Jesus (John 12:20–22).

Andrew is far from the most prominently mentioned apostle in the four Gospel accounts. But his time with Jesus teaches us an important message: being used of God to bring others into His kingdom isn't always a matter of teaching, preaching, or facilitating. Sometimes it's as simple as finding opportunities to bring people to Jesus.

What Did That Man's Name Mean?

Just as today, some biblical names had meanings.
Here are a few of those meanings,
including names of some men in this book.

JABEZ: To grieve

JACOB: Supplanter

JASON: About to cure

JEREMIAH: God will rise

JESUS/JOSHUA: Jehovah saves

JETHRO: His excellence

JOEL: Jehovah is his God

JONAH: A dove

JONATHAN: Jehovah given

JOSEPH: Let him add

JOSIAH: Founded of God

JUDAH: Celebrated

THE CUPBEARER: Too Much Wine, Too Little Appreciation

*And the chief butler told his dream to Joseph, and said to him,
In my dream, behold, a vine was before me; and in the vine
were three branches: and it was as though it budded,
and her blossoms shot forth; and the clusters
thereof brought forth ripe grapes.*

Genesis 40:9-10 KJV

The cupbearer (or chief butler) had annoyed Pharaoh and been thrown in the dungeon. To say he was scared was an understatement. Then he had a weird dream that just added to his worries.

Thankfully, there was a fellow prisoner called Joseph who was willing to ask God to interpret the dream. He reassured the cupbearer that he would soon be free.

The cupbearer had never really understood how good he had it. His exalted position in Pharaoh's court was a blessing. Even the wine he served was a gift from God. But it was only when he lost all that that he was prepared to even listen to God. Joseph asked one favor in return: "Don't forget me!"

But once the good times returned, the cupbearer (temporarily) forgot God and His messenger.

Does that ring any bells? When hard times come along, as they always do, we beg God to help us out. Once restored. . .we forget Him again. Thankfully, the cupbearer finally remembered to help Joseph, but let's not take chances like that. Praise God and remember Him in the good times and the bad because He never forgets us!

SIMON THE PHARISEE:
Forgiveness Well Served

*One of the Pharisees asked Jesus to have dinner with him,
so Jesus went to his home and sat down to eat.*

Luke 7:36 NLT

Pharisees like Simon found it difficult to like Jesus. He healed on the Sabbath, rubbed shoulders with the outcasts, and, frankly knew more than they did. Simon, however, was intrigued, and invited Jesus to his home to learn more about this unconventional teacher.

Immediately Simon found a reason to condemn Jesus. A prostitute knelt at His feet and in tears began to use expensive perfume to clean and anoint His feet. She used her own hair as a washcloth. Didn't Jesus know this woman was a sinner? In the eyes of the Pharisee, you had to be morally superior to be counted worthy of time and attention.

Jesus helped Simon understand that the love the woman showed to Him was based on an understanding of the debt of sin she was being forgiven.

While customary for a host to wash the feet of their guests, it was also customary to greet a guest with a kiss on the cheek and anoint them with olive oil. Simon had failed as a host. However, the sinful woman had done all these things at an incredible personal cost.

We will always find reason to condemn the sin of others, but sin dwells inside us as well. The love we share with others shouldn't be a mere sense of duty. We should love much because we have been forgiven much.

JAMES: Half-brother of Jesus

"It is my judgment, therefore, that we should not make it difficult for the Gentiles who are turning to God."

Acts 15:19 NIV

Try to imagine an older brother who never does anything wrong. He never even runs to tell Mom when you disobey, but helps you see the wisdom of getting back on the right path. He never complains about his chores. It could be worse—your mom probably never says, "Why can't you be like Jesus?"

By the time James and his brothers, Joses, Simon, and Judas, were grown, however, they had decided that Jesus was not the Messiah. They taunted Him about His powers and claims, telling Him He needed to hurry to the Passover Feast in Jerusalem so lots of people could learn about Him. Today they might have said, "You really need to do a YouTube segment!"

But after the crucifixion and resurrection, Jesus made a point of showing Himself to James, who then believed, as did his other brothers and his sisters. When God had freed Peter from prison, Peter made a point of telling those who had prayed for his release to "tell James and the other brethren" the news.

James must have been a careful and diligent student under the apostles' teaching, for in the Acts of the Apostles, we soon find him a respected leader of the church at Jerusalem, and later a writer of God's Word.

OBADIAH: Servant of the Lord

*"I'm not asking you to take them out of the world,
but to keep them safe from the evil one."*

John 17:15 NLT

Obadiah of 1 Kings 18 (not the writer of the Old Testament book of that name) managed the palace of King Ahab and his wife Jezebel. The royal household must have been a treacherous place to work. Ahab did more evil than any of the previous kings of Judah. Jezebel was as evil as her husband and even more devious.

Although he lived in dark times, Obadiah was a devoted follower of the Lord. When Jezebel hunted down prophets of God, Obadiah managed to safely hide one hundred of them in caves and brought them food and water.

During a severe famine, as Obadiah looked for water and grazing land for Ahab's cattle, he met Elijah—a great prophet and very much a wanted man. Elijah instructed Obadiah to tell the king, "Elijah is here." Obadiah at first objected. If the Spirit carried Elijah away, then King Ahab would be furious the prophet had escaped and punish Obadiah instead. Despite his misgivings, however, Obadiah faithfully delivered the message, which led to the dramatic contest on Mount Carmel between Elijah and the prophets of Baal.

Obadiah was a man who loved God more than he feared King Ahab. His example reassures Christians that they, too, can live in the world with a determination to preserve righteousness in the face of evil.

THE HUNGRY LEPERS: Used by God

Now there were four men with leprosy at the entrance of the city
gate. They said to each other, "Why stay here until we die?"

2 Kings 7:3 NIV

With Samaria hunkered down inside its city walls in fear of the Arameans (Syrians), its people were starving. The situation for four Samarian lepers on the outside of the city walls was even more dire. Even if they entered the city, violating the cleanliness laws, they wouldn't find any food. If they went into the camp of the Arameans in search of food, they could be killed. But they took a risk and did so anyway.

They had no idea that God had gone before them, chasing the Arameans out of the camp with the sounds of chariots, horses, and a great army. When they reached the camp and realized that it was abandoned, the lepers ate, drank, and began to store up goods for themselves. Then their conscience got the best of them, prompting them to report their findings to the king so the rest of the city could partake.

God provided for His people through four unclean men who were simply in self-preservation mode, but who had the integrity to do what was right when nobody would have known anything different. As we seek to overcome our own impurity and limitations, we, too, will be faced with the opportunity to do what is right. May we choose well.

ANDREW: Looking for Something More

As Jesus walked beside the Sea of Galilee, he saw Simon and his brother Andrew casting a net into the lake, for they were fishermen. "Come, follow me," Jesus said, "and I will send you out to fish for people." At once they left their nets and followed him.

Mark 1:16-18 NIV

As we read the account of Jesus calling Andrew and his brother Simon (later called Peter), it's impossible to miss how quickly and eagerly they dropped everything and followed Him. Of course, that call came from God in the flesh, so we can understand why they followed.

But was there something else that prepared them to so readily follow Jesus—something a little more "human?" Were they ready because they longed for something more in their lives?

The Bible doesn't tell us much about Andrew and Simon's lives before they began following Jesus. We know they were fisherman, and that they lived in a time when Jewish people eagerly anticipated the arrival of their Messiah. And they had already met Jesus some time earlier along the Jordan River (John 1:35–42). So it's not hard to imagine the brothers talking about Him and about how honored they would feel if He called them to give up their lives of fishing to join Him.

When that call came, both men were more than ready to drop their nets and follow. Has God put on your heart something greater, something of more eternal significance, than what you're doing now? If you believe He has, then you need to be ready to drop everything and move out when He calls, "Follow Me."

DEMETRIUS: Delivering More Than Just Mail

Demetrius is well spoken of by everyone—
and even by the truth itself. We also speak well of him,
and you know that our testimony is true.

3 John 12 NIV

Demetrius probably wasn't just a letter carrier for the apostle John. He was probably active in other aspects of the early church and just happened to be providing this humble but important service.

But there is one extraordinary thing we do know about him. No one had a bad word to say about him. No one. Even "the truth," which we might take as the Holy Spirit saying good things about him.

Think about the people you know and ask yourself how common that is. Even genuinely good people have their critics (which has more to do with the critics than the people they talk about).

In the letter John is reminding Gaius not to imitate evil but good. He says that those who do good are from God. He then goes on to commend Demetrius. From that we can only surmise that Demetrius spent his time doing good.

In doing good we must of necessity put others before ourselves. In removing ourselves as far as possible from the equation, we leave less that can be criticized, filling the space with God and works that no one can complain about.

It seems that in the early church even the mail carriers were expected to set a good example.

SETH: The Son of Replacement

When Adam had lived 130 years, he had a son in his own likeness, in his own image; and he named him Seth.

Genesis 5:3 NIV

Seth was the third son of Adam and Eve—at least the third one mentioned. Among his descendants was Enoch (whom God took to heaven without him dying), Methuselah (who lived 969 years), and Noah (who built the ark). Even Jesus is linked to the line of Seth.

The Bible is clear that when Cain killed Abel it was Seth who would be a sort of replacement son for Adam and Eve. The act of murder left one son in the ground and another estranged from his family. The birth of Seth almost seems like a new start to parenting for the first couple.

Seth was 912 years old when he died. If we were to put together a timeline, it is possible that Noah knew this multiple great-grandfather.

Little more is known about Seth, but the details related to where he came from and who was part of his family line were important to the story of his life. So it's easy to consider that Seth took what he learned about God from his parents and intentionally passed it along.

If you grew up in a Christian home, use what you know to continue impacting your family for Jesus. If your upbringing wasn't Christian, use what you're learning about Jesus now to begin to impact future generations.

JACOB: Helping God Along

*Esau asked, "What's the meaning of all these flocks and
herds I met?" "To find favor in your eyes, my lord," he said.
But Esau said, "I already have plenty, my brother.
Keep what you have for yourself."*

Genesis 33:8-9 NIV

Shortly after Jacob stole the blessing from Esau, his mother
heard Esau say that after his father's death, he would kill
Jacob. Mom then tells Dad that it will be the death of her
if Jacob marries a Canaanite woman, as Esau has. So Isaac
tells Jacob to get on up to Padan Aram and marry one of his
mother's nieces.

Once there, however, Jacob meets his match in his uncle
Laban and ends up married to two of Laban's daughters. He
wanted the younger, but was tricked into taking the elder
first. (How do you like that, Mr. Birthright-Stealer?)

Jacob doesn't shun trickery because of this lesson. He
agrees to work longer for Laban in exchange for all the
spotted animals of the herds he has been tending. Then
he puts spotted sticks in view of all the breeding animals,
believing they will bear spotted offspring. They do, but only
because God causes it.

Jacob goes on manipulating until, traveling back to his
homeland, he divides up his people to suffer the least losses
if Esau and his people attack. But Esau is glad to see him.

Now, consider: did Jacob need to manipulate events to
bring about the promises God had made?

NICODEMUS: Progression of Belief

"Rabbi," he said, "we all know that God has sent you to teach us. Your miraculous signs are evidence that God is with you."

John 3:2 NLT

Nicodemus was a religious leader, a Pharisee, and a member of the ruling Jewish Sanhedrin. He appears three times in the Gospel of John, and each event shows his growing awareness that Jesus was the Son of God.

The first time he comes to Jesus at night, and Jesus tells him of the necessity of being born of the water and the Spirit. Nicodemus's question of how to be "born again" elicits the most quoted verse of the New Testament: "For God so loved the world. . ." (John 3:16 NIV).

When Nicodemus is next mentioned, he advises the Sanhedrin to avoid rash action against Jesus. "Is it legal to convict a man before he is given a hearing?" (John 7:51 NLT).

After the crucifixion of Jesus, Nicodemus supplies myrrh and aloes to anoint the body of Jesus. With Joseph of Arimathea's help, he puts the body in an unused, empty tomb (John 19:39, 41).

Some people become suddenly aware of their need for a Savior. Others, like Nicodemus, follow a progression of a questioning mind, an acceptance, and finally full belief of the most quoted verse: "He gave his one and only Son, that whoever believes in him shall not perish but have eternal life."

What Did That Man's Name Mean?

Just as today, some biblical names had meanings.
Here are a few of those meanings,
including names of some men in this book.

KADMIEL: Presence of God

KALLAI: Frivolous

KEDAR: Dusky

KENAZ: Hunter

KISHI: War, battle

KOHATH: Allied

KORAH: To make bald

LABAN: To be white or to make bricks

LAPIDOTH: To shine, or a lamp or flame

LEHABIM: Flames

LEVI: Attached

LIBNI: White

LEVI: From Violence to Priesthood

Three days later, while all of them were still in pain, two of Jacob's sons, Simeon and Levi, Dinah's brothers, took their swords and attacked the unsuspecting city, killing every male.

Genesis 34:25 NIV

When Jacob's sons learned that their sister, Dinah, had been raped by Shechem, son of Hamor the Hivite, and that Hamor had approached their father to ask for Dinah's hand in marriage for the offender, they stepped in and gave Shechem a condition—every male must be circumcised so the Shechemites would be like them.

They did, and as they were healing, Levi, the eleventh-born son of Jacob, and his brother Simeon killed every male in the city, taking all of their wealth as well as their women and children (verse 29). In so doing, Jacob feared that Simeon and Levi brought trouble and possible retribution to his household.

Levi reacted to the news of his sister's rape out of emotion rather than righteousness. Later, on Jacob's deathbed, he cursed Simeon and Levi's uncontrolled anger (Genesis 49:5).

Yet God later appointed the tribe of Levi (Numbers 1:50) as His priests—to be set apart for His ministry. No violence or wrongdoing is beyond the redeeming hand of God. If you're hesitant to believe that an acquaintance with a heinous past can receive divine mercy, consider the tribe of Levi. God is in the business of making all things new.

AQUILA: A Radical Approach to His Ministry

[Apollos] began to speak boldly in the synagogue. When Priscilla and Aquila heard him, they invited him to their home and explained to him the way of God more adequately.

Acts 18:26 NIV

Aquila, an important teacher of the Gospel message mentioned several times in the New Testament, had what was during his time a radical approach to his ministry—and to his marriage.

Aquila and his wife, Priscilla, traveled with the apostle Paul, established a church in their home in Ephesus (1 Corinthians 16:19), and taught and trained a Jewish teacher named Apollos, who went on to become a powerful preacher of the Gospel. They were amazing examples of hospitality, of passion for Christ, of passing along what they had learned about the Gospel message to others, and of encouraging new believers in the faith.

Aquila's ministry was powerful and very practical. So what was so radical about it? It was radical in that it involved his wife, Priscilla, who appears to be an equal partner in all he did—and this at a time when the society (the first-century Roman Empire) didn't see women as equal to men.

It probably wasn't by accident that when Priscilla and Aquila are mentioned in the New Testament, the name of the wife is mentioned first nearly every time. That didn't mean the New Testament writers intended to place Priscilla in a place in front of her husband. It simply meant that in God's eyes, men and women are of equal value in building His kingdom and spreading His message of salvation.

DANIEL: With Christ Before Jesus

And he said unto me, O Daniel, a man greatly beloved,
understand the words that I speak unto thee, and stand upright:
for unto thee am I now sent. And when he had spoken
this word unto me, I stood trembling.

Daniel 10:11 KJV

As Daniel's story was proceeding, as he refused to eat the king's food, as he continued to pray, as he faced the lions in their den, and as he became a powerful man, another even more dramatic story was unfolding.

When Nebuchadnezzar had a disturbing dream, Daniel asked God for the meaning behind it. He seemed to have gotten a bit more than he imagined. God told him the meaning, but a series of prophetic visions must have begun that often left Daniel exhausted. It's generally considered that those visions told of the rise and fall of four empires, predicted the Messiah, and described the end times. The figure in white and gold who told Gabriel to explain these things to Daniel seems to have been Jesus Himself.

No wonder it often took the prophet a week to recover!

If Daniel tells us anything, it is that God will give us way more than we ask for, if we ask in faith and love. He also gives us the best answer to the question, "When will the end times be?" The answer is, in effect, "Don't you worry about that. Just go on your way, and prepare for your inheritance" (Daniel 12:13, paraphrased).

SERGIUS PAULUS: Redeemed from False Teaching

When the governor saw what had happened, he became a believer, for he was astonished at the teaching about the Lord.

Acts 13:12 NLT

The apostle Paul was on his first missionary journey. He arrived on the island of Cyprus where he met a sorcerer/false prophet known by two names, Bar-Jesus and Elymas. If it sounds like Paul discovered a spiritual circus in Cyprus, that's probably because it bore a remarkable resemblance.

In the midst of this roadside attraction was governor Sergius Paulus, who is described as an intelligent man. In spite of the sorcerer's protests, Sergius Paulus was interested in hearing Paul speak. It just so happens Paul had messages from God for both the governor and the sorcerer. Elymas did everything he could to corrupt the content of the message for Sergius Paulus. When he did, the sorcerer received his message—blindness, for "perverting the true ways of the Lord." This miracle was used by God to bring the governor to faith in Christ.

God can always be trusted to deliver His message. Just because someone lives in an environment that seems unwelcoming to a testimony of faith, we should never believe that that they are incapable of understanding and believing the good news we share. When we're willing to communicate the best news we've ever heard we may be surprised where God might allow us to speak.

JOASH: Fear No False God

Therefore on that day he called him Jerubbaal, saying, Let Baal plead against him, because he hath thrown down his altar.

Judges 6:32 KJV

When Gideon obeyed God by destroying his father's idol to Baal, he did it at night to avoid interference.

The next day, men of the area mobbed the farm and demanded that Gideon be killed for what he had done to their god.

But Gideon's father, Joash, was a practical and wise man. Although he had owned the image of Baal, he seems to have turned from any faith in the idol. Perhaps he had been thinking of Baal's powerlessness for some time—and the moment he saw the destruction, he had all the proof he needed.

Joash threw a taunt back at the mob, demanding that anyone who pleaded for Baal should be killed, not Gideon. Seeing that Baal had no power to protect himself, what kind of a god was he? Joash said, "Let Baal plead his own case." It was a very clever defense, and it worked. The local farmers couldn't come up with an answer to that one.

NEHEMIAH: Rebuilding Walls, Rebuilding Faith

The king asked, "Well, how can I help you?" With a prayer to the God of heaven, I replied, "If it please the king, and if you are pleased with me, your servant, send me to Judah to rebuild the city where my ancestors are buried."

Nehemiah 2:4–5 NLT

While working in the court of Artaxerxes, king of Persia, Nehemiah learned that the walls of Jerusalem were still in disrepair. Artaxerxes released Nehemiah to put the city in order.

Nehemiah's success is often used as a pattern for effective leadership. He had a passion for the job, he inspected the walls thoroughly, he formulated a plan, and inspired others to do the work. He developed a team of workers, guards, and watchmen, and gave each family a certain section of the wall to rebuild. When presented in this way, the entire story can be told devoid of any spiritual context.

To do so, however, would miss a vital part of the book. Nehemiah is a book about prayer and about a trusting relationship with God. Nehemiah prayed about the problem while in Persia, while restoring the city, and at the end of the effort. He didn't stop there. The nation of Israel had been shattered by foes without and sins within. He also rebuilt the faith of his people. After finishing the walls, he then turned (with Ezra) to rebuilding the spiritual strength of his people.

Successful leadership begins with an authentic prayer life.

LUKE: The Man of Many Talents

*Our dear friend Luke, the doctor,
and Demas send greetings.*
Colossians 4:14 NIV

Luke, the author of the Gospel of Luke and the book of Acts, was a Greek physician from Antioch who became a Christian and later accompanied Paul on his missionary travels, as evidenced by the verse above (see also 2 Timothy 4:11 and Philemon 1:24). Tradition holds that he was also a painter, with some paintings attributed to him still in existence, including "Black Madonna of Częstochowa," housed at a monastery in Poland, and "Salvation of the Roman People" at the Basilica of St. Mary Major in Rome.

As a writer, physician, missionary, and possibly a painter, he would have been an observer—someone who pays special attention to detail. Good creative types of all sorts feel an obligation to depict truth as accurately as possible. It should be no surprise that we read such a person's inspired account of the birth of our Savior from Luke 2 every Christmas, including Mary's personal testimony of the events that day.

Maybe God has wired you to be a creative type, or maybe you're more analytical, or a visionary, or have some other dominant personality trait. However you're wired, evaluate how well you're using those traits for God's glory. And then get to work.

BELSHAZZAR: Ignoring Lessons from the Past

"But you, Belshazzar, his son, have not humbled yourself, though you knew all this. Instead, you have set yourself up against the Lord of heaven. . . . You did not honor the God who holds in his hand your life and all your ways."

Daniel 5:22–23 NIV

There are few things more foolish than refusing to learn lessons from the failings of those who have gone before us. Belshazzar, the Babylonian king, knew well of the dramatic humbling of his grandfather Nebuchadnezzar's pride. Yet his own arrogance somehow led him to believe that he could engage in this sin but with different results.

How wrong he was!

Belshazzar was filled with pride. And like his grandfather, he refused to honor God, but instead celebrated his own power.

Belshazzar knew about the consequences of his grandfather's own arrogance. But instead of applying the lessons of Nebuchadnezzar's fall, he chose to walk down the same path. At the end of his life, a humbled Nebuchadnezzar praised the one true God. But Belshazzar's life didn't end nearly so well.

The Bible tells us that the failures of God's people are recorded in the pages of scripture both as examples and warnings to us today (1 Corinthians 10:1–11). The same thing could easily be said of the failures and sins we see among our friends and family members.

Sadly, Belshazzar's pride kept him from learning a vital lesson from his grandfather's arrogance. We should be careful not to make the same kind of mistake.

DIONYSIUS: A Useful Man to Know

Some of the people became followers of Paul and believed.
Among them was Dionysius, a member of the Areopagus,
also a woman named Damaris, and a number of others.

Acts 17:34 NIV

It seems the people of Athens were very keen on hearing about and discussing the latest ideas. In that kind of setting, ideas very rarely get turned into realities because there is always a new notion waiting to take the place of the previous one. Talking tends to be all that gets done.

Paul was brought before the Areopagus (also known as Mars Hill) to explain this strange new faith he was so keen on spreading. The Areopagus was the equivalent of the High Court, or a religious Senate. Those in attendance would have been very important men in Athenian society.

Most of them would have been curious, but too busy to take this wandering Christian seriously. He may have been an interesting distraction, but they had their own set ideas. Of course, Paul went nowhere under his own will. He wasn't there to entertain bored wealthy men. God knew there was at least one there who was tired of philosophies and wanted truth. That man was Dionysius.

He wasn't the only convert Paul left in that city of many gods when he moved on. . .but the others in the fledgling church must surely have appreciated having an influential ruler on their side!

SIMON OF CYRENE:
Unexpected Burden Bearer

A passerby named Simon, who was from Cyrene,
was coming in from the countryside just then,
and the soldiers forced him to carry Jesus' cross.

Mark 15:21 NLT

It was the time of Passover. Jerusalem was much busier than usual. Simon, a man of Cyrene, had just arrived with his two sons, Alexander and Rufus. The streets were full of people intent on viewing a very specific event. The crowd divided for a man being led to a hill just outside town where He would be crucified. This man, Jesus, was carrying His own cross, but he was severely wounded and struggled under the weight.

An impatient soldier grabbed Simon and forced him to carry the cross for the condemned man. We don't know if he exchanged words with Jesus, and we don't know how this forced labor affected Simon's sons. However, it's widely believed that his son Rufus became a leader in the early church (Romans 16:13).

Anyone who came in contact with Jesus was given opportunity to change their life direction, from the woman at the well to the Pharisee, Nicodemus. In those moments when Simon shouldered the weight of the cross used to kill the Son of God, we are left with questions of how such an encounter would change a man.

In recalling the man Simon, we may remember our own first connection with a risen Savior and how that changed the course of our lives.

What Did That Man's Name Mean?

Just as today, some biblical names had meanings.
Here are a few of those meanings,
including names of some men in this book.

MACHIR: Salesman

MAGPIASH: Exterminator of the moth

MALACHI: Ministrative

MAMRE: Lusty, vigorous

MANASSEH: Causing to forget

MATTATHIAS: Gift of God

MELCHIZEDEK: King of right

METHUSELAH: Man of a dart

MICHAEL: Who is like God?

MIDIAN: Brawling, contentious

MOSES: Drawing out (of the water), rescued

MUSHI: Sensitive

JAMES, SON OF ZEBEDEE:
Enthusiasm to Spare

*And when his disciples James and John saw this, they said,
Lord, wilt thou that we command fire to come down
from heaven, and consume them, even as Elias did?*

Luke 9:54 KJV

Among the disciples of Jesus, Peter usually gets the notoriety for speaking before thinking. But in the citation above, James (with his brother, John) asks a rash question that reaps a rebuke from the Lord. Jesus tells them that they don't know the Spirit they belong to.

Their question seems similar to the attitude of new soldiers who are sometimes described as "Gung ho!" They want to bring all available power to bear on a conflict that might not require that strong a response.

During his years under the Master's teaching, James was privileged to see the raising of Jairus's daughter, the transfiguration, and Jesus' spiritual agony in the garden of Gethsemane.

But Jesus gave James and John the title "Sons of Thunder"—or in the sense of the Aramaic word Jesus used, "sons of commotion!" This was not a compliment. Jesus was pointing out their tendency to raise a ruckus when a calm response would be better.

John doesn't seem to fit the description because we have his gentle writings from later in life. Perhaps James would have softened as well, had not Herod Agrippa executed him for political reasons. But he was the first apostle to die for his faith and to be again in the presence of Jesus.

NIMROD: Rise and Fall

Cush was the father of Nimrod,
who became a mighty warrior on earth.
1 Chronicles 1:10 NIV

Nimrod was a great-grandson of Noah. For a time, he was admired: People would say, "This man is like Nimrod, the greatest hunter in the world" (Genesis 10:9 NLT). Then he became a formidable ruler: he built a kingdom in Babylonia and several cities including Nineveh (Genesis 10:10, 11). Finally, he became intensely reviled: Joel describes the countries of Israel's enemies as the "gates of Nimrod."

Where did Nimrod go wrong? Chapter 10 of Genesis says the descendants of Noah were spread over various lands. Chapter 11 tells why they scattered. On the plains of Shinar they began building a city with a tower to reach the heavens. They didn't construct the tower for the glory of their Creator but to make a name for themselves. Before the tower was completed, God confused their speech and scattered them. The place where they started the tower became known as Babylon, from Babel, meaning confusion.

Unlike his great-grandfather who built the Ark to save himself and his family, and then after the Flood built an altar to sacrifice to God, Nimrod built cities to make a name for himself. He had a great impact during his time, but today his story occupies a minor part in the Bible. His name is mentioned only four times. Greatness comes from honoring God and serving others.

MALCHUS: Healed by Christ

*Then Simon Peter, who had a sword, drew it
and struck the high priest's servant, cutting off his
right ear. (The servant's name was Malchus.)*

John 18:10 NIV

You're the servant of the high priest, and he instructs you to accompany him and a detachment of soldiers, along with the chief priests, Pharisees, and a man who has turned against Jesus. You are going to seize Jesus. When you arrive, however, He speaks and the power of His words knocks you to the ground, giving you the sense that He is more than just a man (verse 6).

After you get up, one of His servants draws a sword and slices off your right ear. As surprised as you are, you're even more stunned by what Jesus says and does next: "'No more of this!' And he touched the man's ear and healed him" (Luke 22:51).

Malchus is never mentioned again in scripture, so we don't know what sort of spiritual impact Jesus' actions made on him, but surely he must have wondered whether the charges against Jesus were false. What type of blasphemer shows concern and compassion for his enemies?

Is one of your enemies being mistreated by someone who is "on your side"? If so, ask your ally to stand down and then reach out to the mistreated in a way that may win him or her over.

AGABUS: Speaking the Truth

Coming over to us, he took Paul's belt, tied his own hands and feet with it and said, "The Holy Spirit says, 'In this way the Jewish leaders in Jerusalem will bind the owner of this belt and will hand him over to the Gentiles.'"

Acts 21:11 NIV

Agabus was an early New Testament-era prophet who was a picture of courage. He appears for the second time in Acts 21, when he acts in a very strange manner and then announces that the Jewish religious leadership would arrest the apostle Paul in Jerusalem and then hand him over to the Romans.

That couldn't have been an easy message to speak, and Agabus had to know it wouldn't be well received among those who loved the apostle Paul and worked with him. But while he could have "soft sold" the message God had given him—or at least possibly spoken it to Paul privately so as to avoid anguish in the part of his friends—he courageously and openly spoke the truth God had given him to speak.

You may never be faced with a situation in which God has given you a difficult message specifically for someone you know. But you can still follow the example of the prophet Agabus and speak the truth and the whole truth—lovingly and gently—to people God has placed in your life.

DAVID: After God's Forgiving Heart

One evening David got up from his bed and walked around on the roof of the palace. From the roof he saw a woman bathing. The woman was very beautiful, and David sent someone to find out about her. The man said, "She is Bathsheba, the daughter of Eliam and the wife of Uriah the Hittite."

2 Samuel 11:2–3 NIV

David was one of the greatest heroes of the Bible and a man after God's heart. But, let's face it, when he had a man killed so he could take his wife, he failed big time.

Uriah the Hittite was a good man and a loyal soldier. He didn't deserve to die because another man couldn't control his passions. Bathsheba didn't deserve to be made a widow by her king.

Of course, God didn't let him get away with such horrendous acts. He had put himself and his desires before his duty. There had to be consequences. It's a measure of the man that, having fallen short, David took his punishment, went straight back to serving God, and was, no doubt, welcomed enthusiastically into heaven when he died.

In many ways David was a wonderful example of a man of faith. He showed us how to live as a man after God's heart. But he wasn't perfect. None of us are, of course, but David's imperfection teaches us one more thing about God. It seems He has a big heart for flawed people.

SHEPHERDS: Offering the Gift of Praise

The shepherds went back to their flocks,
glorifying and praising God for all they had heard
and seen. It was just as the angel had told them.
Luke 2:20 NLT

The angels arrived with unprecedented news. God was sending His Son, Jesus, to our world as a baby. Most people would find it hard to believe, but in a stable in Bethlehem Jesus was born. There were no news crews filming and interviewing, no special living arrangements were made, and no congratulatory letters or postcards arrived.

Instead God sent His angels to bring this eternity-altering news to shepherds. The lowliest of occupations viewed shepherds as a step down in social class.

Who wouldn't be frightened if, when you're watching for threats to the sheep, an angel drops by to let you know that Jesus had been born and you were to go and see the new king. That didn't happen a lot.

There probably weren't questions about what gift to bring. The shepherds were simply compelled to go for a visit and let their presence be a gift. When it was over they told others about Jesus, but the Bible doesn't seem to suggest that others paid attention to them.

Jesus came for everyone. The gift the shepherds brought was praise, and their example speaks volumes to us today. When you encounter Jesus, let worship be your gift.

JETHRO: Wise Father-in-Law

And Moses' father in law said unto him,
The thing that thou doest is not good.

Exodus 18:17 KJV

Moses' father-in-law, Jethro, traveled from his home area to bring his daughter Zipporah and her two sons back to Moses. After a joyful meeting, Moses told Jethro all that God had done to Egypt's pharaoh and for Israel. Jethro praised God and recognized that He was above all other gods.

When Jethro saw all the judicial work Moses had to do every day, he realized that the effort was too much for one man. Moses sat before the people and settled disputes all day, every day but the Sabbath.

Jethro told him he should appoint leaders over groups of one thousand, one hundred, fifty, and ten. Further, Moses should continue to teach the people the laws of God, but let the leaders settle all but the most important disputes—which Moses would handle. These new leaders, Jethro said, should be men "such as fear God, men of truth, hating covetousness."

Moses immediately acted on Jethro's advice.

This wise change of procedure was only possible because Moses and Jethro had a long relationship of trust and respect. When Moses returned to Egypt to lead Israel out, it seems he sent Zipporah and his sons to Jethro for safekeeping, showing that Moses and Jethro already trusted each other. Jethro showed himself worthy of that trust when he brought them back safely.

After God, family and friends are our greatest help.

PAUL: Persistence of Vision

*And I am convinced that nothing
can ever separate us from God's love.*
Romans 8:38 NLT

Paul's early life was filled with Jewish law and tradition. Although born in Tarsus, he'd been brought up and educated in Jerusalem under Gamaliel, a well-known Jewish scholar. Whatever he had intended after this education, his life changed suddenly when Jesus spoke to him on the road to Damascus. He then began a remarkable new journey.

During his second missionary trip, Paul received a message from God in the form of a vision of a man calling him to Macedonia. After evangelizing Greece and Asia Minor, he wanted to visit Rome, the chief city of the Gentile world. By the end of his third missionary journey, however, he still had not done so.

He returned to Jerusalem where a series of events—an arrest, three trials, and a shipwreck—ended with the chief apostle to the Gentiles in Rome. He lived in a private house with a Roman guard, but no one stopped him from preaching, writing, and receiving visitors.

Some lives follow a straight-as-an-arrow path from first effort to final success. Other lives follow a long and winding path in which the end may not be in sight or even obvious. Even with an unseen goal we can take comfort in the fact that a Christian who follows a persistent vision under God's guidance will arrive at a satisfying resolution.

MATTHIAS: The Replacement

"Therefore it is necessary to choose one of the men who have been with us the whole time the Lord Jesus was living among us, beginning from John's baptism to the time when Jesus was taken up from us. For one of these must become a witness with us of his resurrection."

Acts 1:21–22 NIV

Matthias saw Jesus' ministry firsthand, from His baptism, to His miracles, to His ascension. However, he had no idea that he might one day be one of the twelve apostles, all of whom had been chosen by Jesus. But then Judas hanged himself.

After Jesus' ascension, and then much prayer by his 120 followers, the apostle Peter recognized that Psalm 109:8 prophesied a replacement for Judas, so they prayed and cast lots on two candidates: Joseph called Barsabbas (also known as Justus), and Matthias. The lot fell Matthias' way and he was added to the eleven.

While Matthias is not mentioned again in the New Testament after Acts 1, a number of traditions regarding him exist, including one that says he preached the Gospel in Judea before being martyred. The Book of Common Prayer celebrates his life on February 24, offering the following prayer: "Grant that your Church, being delivered from false apostles, may always be guided and governed by faithful and true pastors. . ."

Notice how much prayer was given, both by the apostles and modern Christians, regarding the purity of Christ's church. Is that something you pray about?

BALAAM: A Prophet Who Lacked a Heart for God

Then the LORD opened the donkey's mouth, and it
said to Balaam, "What have I done to you
to make you beat me these three times?"

Numbers 22:28 NIV

Balaam, a soothsayer whose story is told in Numbers 22–24, is best known as the man took a tongue-lashing from. . .his donkey. But Balaam's story is a complicated one. He spoke three blessings on the people of Israel (Numbers 23), and he even uttered a prophecy of the coming Messiah (Numbers 24:15–19).

Sounds like Balaam was a true prophet and man of God, doesn't it? But other Bible passages denounce him severely. In the Old Testament, he is called out for practicing soothsaying, which the Law of Moses condemned, and other passages suggest that he had asked God for permission to curse Israel. In the New Testament, the apostle Peter refers to him as one "who loved the wages of wickedness" (2 Peter 2:15 NIV). And Jesus condemned him as one who taught Balak, the Midianite king who wanted Balaam to curse the Israelites, "to put a stumbling block before the children of Israel" (Revelation 2:14 NKJV).

The lesson we can take from the life of Balaam is that God cares far more about our hearts than He does about our gifts or outward actions. Balaam was a prophet who had the ability to bless those God wanted to bless. But he didn't have a heart for God, and in the end his lack of true devotion to the Lord sealed his doom.

What Did That Man's Name Mean?

Just as today, some biblical names had meanings.
Here are a few of those meanings,
including names of some men in this book.

NAHOR: Snorer

NAHUM: Comfortable

NAPHTALI: My wrestling

NATHAN: Given

NEHEMIAH: Consolation of God

NERIAH: Light of God

NICODEMUS: Victorious among his
people

NOAH: Rest

OBADIAH: Serving God

ONESIMUS: Profitable

OREB: Mosquito

OTHNIEL: Force of God

ELI: Good Dad, Bad Dad

*In that day I will perform against Eli all things
which I have spoken concerning his house:
when I begin, I will also make an end.*

1 Samuel 3:12 KJV

Judges led Israel before the coming of the kings, but though Eli the high priest served God for forty years, he wasn't named as a judge. He acted nobly at first but turned a blind eye to injustices as he grew older. Most of these injustices had to do with his sons who were abusing the women of the temple and helping themselves to the offering. When Eli discovered what was happening, he rebuked them—sort of—but he spared the rod and spoiled his whole bloodline. As a punishment God made sure the line of Eli would die or be made subservient from his generation onward.

He was not a total failure, though. Eli wasn't such a good father to his own sons, but he was a good foster father to Samuel, a young boy who was given as an offering to Yahweh. He raised the boy in an atmosphere of faith, and Samuel went on to become the last of the judges and the first of the major prophets since Moses.

Eli obviously knew how to raise boys (and priests), but when it came to his own sons his standards lowered considerably. In the end, he did them no favors.

One standard of Fatherhood applies throughout life. And it's not ours—it's God's.

SIMEON: The Wait was Over

Moved by the Spirit, he went into the temple courts.
When the parents brought in the child Jesus to do
for him what the custom of the Law required,
Simeon took him in his arms and praised God.
Luke 2:27–28 NIV

Mary and Joseph prepared themselves and their baby to go to the temple for purification. While the couple made their way through the crowds, another man was urged by the Holy Spirit to enter the temple courts. Like other citizens in Jerusalem, Simeon had been waiting for the arrival of the Messiah, but unlike the others he had been promised that he wouldn't die until the Messiah arrived.

When Simeon saw Jesus, he held Him and prayed, "Sovereign Lord, as you have promised, you may now dismiss your servant in peace. For my eyes have seen your salvation" (Luke 2:29–30 NIV).

Mary and Joseph were stunned by Simeon's prayer, but then the old man indicated there would be many difficulties in the future for both Jesus and Mary.

The Bible doesn't tell us when Simeon passed away, but he lived and died with the promise that he would see the Messiah. Simeon was among the first to recognize the infant Jesus for who He really was.

Every day we have the opportunity to either remember who Jesus is and allow that knowledge to alter how we live, or set Him aside in a failure to recognize today's greatest blessings.

THE PHILIPPIAN JAILER:
Finding Salvation

*[He] brought them out, and said, Sirs, what must I do to be
saved? And they said, Believe on the Lord Jesus Christ, and thou
shalt be saved, and thy house. And they spake unto him the word
of the Lord, and to all that were in his house. . . . And when he
had brought them into his house, he set meat before them,
and rejoiced, believing in God with all his house.*

Acts 16:30–34 KJV

The jailer at Philippi was sleeping soundly while Paul and
Silas sang praises to God at midnight. But God caused an
earthquake that left him wide awake and terrified. All the
locked prison doors swung open and all the prisoners were
freed of their constraints. Since his own blood would be shed
if they escaped, he probably saw his life flash before his eyes.

Paul and Silas clearly answered the jailer's plea to tell
him how to be saved. Whether he first wanted to be saved
from the wrath of God or of Rome is left unsaid. But after
they explained what Jesus had done, he believed in the
saving power of the crucified and risen Messiah of the Jews.

It's notable that while Paul and Silas spoke to the
jailer about what Jesus had done, the Bible tells us that he
"rejoiced, believing in God"—a clear, if seldom-recognized
proof text that Jesus is God in the flesh.

NOAH: Walking with God

*Noah was a righteous man, the only blameless person living
on earth at the time, and he walked in close fellowship with God.*
Genesis 6:9 NLT

The Bible lists Noah as a hero of faith and explains that
he built the ark despite the fact that a worldwide flood had
never happened before (Hebrews 11:7). God gave specific
instructions, which Noah followed exactly in building the
ark and bringing the animals inside. His efforts showed
unparalleled determination as he was mocked for years
while building the ark. He had victory over impossible
circumstances because he obeyed God and saved himself,
his wife, his three sons, and their three wives.

Once the floodwaters receded, God commanded the
family to leave the ark, and they did that. Noah's first action
was to build an altar and make a sacrifice to the Lord. The
world started afresh with a leader who "walked with God."
In Noah's evil time he could not walk in fellowship with
others because they were given over to sin. Instead he had
fellowship with God. He exhibited faithfulness, patience,
and persistence. Noah demonstrated that a person could
remain loyal to God even in the heart of a dark and corrupt
world.

A person's character is reflected by those with whom
he walks. By walking and talking with God we become
more like Him and less like the world that seeks to make us
conform to sinful ways.

MEN OF FAITH: Find a Way

And they came, bringing to him [Jesus] a paralytic carried
by four men. And when they could not get near him
because of the crowd, they removed the roof above
him, and when they had made an opening,
they let down the bed on which the paralytic lay.

Mark 2:3–4 ESV

The word about Jesus' ability to heal the sick had spread to the point that when He returned to Peter's house after a trip through Galilee (where He had recently healed a leper), a large crowd gathered outside, hoping for an encounter with Jesus.

By the time the four men and their paralyzed friend arrived, they couldn't get him near enough to the door, so they removed a portion of the roof and lowered him at Jesus' feet. He responded in a remarkable way: "When Jesus saw their faith, he said to the paralyzed man, 'Son, your sins are forgiven' " (verse 5 NIV). By referencing "their faith," Jesus saw the four men and their friend as a collective unit (a spiritual superteam, if you will) who exercised their faith in His ability to forgive and ultimately heal.

A supernatural power that this world cannot understand, or often accept, occurs whenever two or three are gathered in Christ's name. For in this circumstance, Christ dwells. Do you have a group of spiritual brothers who share your faith? Are you willing to tear the roof off a spiritual barrier for one another?

APOLLOS: A Profile in Humility and Teachability

Meanwhile a Jew named Apollos, a native of Alexandria,
came to Ephesus. He was a learned man,
with a thorough knowledge of the Scriptures.

Acts 18:24 NIV

This might be generalizing a bit, but the best educated and most knowledgeable among us aren't always—or even usually—the humblest or most teachable. After all, they're the ones with the knowledge and who most often have the ability to impart that knowledge to others.

The Bible describes Apollos, a teacher who would become a friend of the apostle Paul, as a well-educated man who knew his Bible. We first meet him after he traveled from Alexandria (a major center of learning in Egypt) to Ephesus, where he began teaching with great passion in the synagogue.

Apollos certainly had a lot of knowledge, and he also had a desire to teach people about Jesus. But the Bible tells us that his knowledge of the Gospel message was incomplete. Then he met a married couple named Priscilla and Aquila, who took him into their home and became what we would call his mentors.

Apollos, who humbly and eagerly soaked in Priscilla and Aquila's teaching, was soon ready to preach and defend the message of salvation through Jesus more completely and more effectively (Acts 18:27–28).

Someone once said, "I don't know everything, but I know a lot more than nothing. And I am willing to learn what God wants me to learn." This is a humble attitude we should share with Apollos.

ELIJAH: All the Way with the Lord

And after six days Jesus taketh Peter, James, and John his brother, and bringeth them up into an high mountain apart, and was transfigured before them: and his face did shine as the sun, and his raiment was white as the light. And, behold, there appeared unto them Moses and Elias talking with him.

Matthew 17:1–3 KJV

Elijah is one of the few figures in the Bible who seem to transcend ordinary life. As if his work on earth wasn't spectacular enough, this man seems to have kept busy even after he was taken up to heaven. The Jewish people fully expected him to return, and both John the Baptist and Jesus were suspected of being the returned prophet.

Elijah and Moses also appeared at the transfiguration of Jesus. As the three met (and shone) on the top of a high mountain, the disciples saw them deep in conversation. Elijah was still deeply involved in the Lord's work even centuries after his departure. Peter actually seems to have interrupted them to suggest building shelters.

In the book of Malachi, Elijah is promised as the herald of that "great and terrible day" when Christ comes back in all His glory. So his work apparently isn't done yet.

Now, that's how to be a servant of God. . .walking so closely with Him that life and the afterlife blend seamlessly into one!

SIMON THE SORCERER:
Equal Opportunity Deception

*A man named Simon had been a sorcerer there for many years,
amassing the people of Samaria and claiming to be someone great.*

Acts 8:9 NLT

Like "Oz the Magnificent," the sorcerer named Simon had
followers, but could do nothing on his own. He relied on
spiritual powers he didn't understand to amaze, astound, and
impress. When Philip came to preach the Gospel in Samaria,
Simon paid close attention to a message he recognized as
powerful, and if there was power in the message perhaps he
could add it to his collection.

When Peter and John came to town, Simon saw God's
power demonstrated through the gift of the Holy Spirit.
This demonstration seemed like a new opportunity to the
Samaritan sorcerer. Being an equal opportunity deceiver, he
offered Peter and John a cash bonus saying, "Let me have this
power, too, so that when I lay my hands on people, they will
receive the Holy Spirit!"

The disciples considered him a wicked, confused sinner
and made it clear the Holy Spirit wasn't for sale. They went
so far as to declare Simon's money should perish with him.
Simon suddenly believed he needed prayer. He had finally
encountered something more powerful than anything he
had known, and he shrunk in the presence of the true power
of God.

Our faith can't be sold or transferred. It is the personal
and transforming power of God available to all.

JOASH, THE KING: A Follower at Heart

*And Jehoiada and his sons anointed him,
and said, God save the king.*

2 Chronicles 23:11 KJV

Thanks to Joash's aunt Jehosheba, the wife of Jehoiada, he escaped being murdered by the skin of his teeth—if he had any teeth at less than one year old.

Queen Athaliah thought she had killed all the heirs to the throne of her son, Ahaziah. By the way, those heirs happened to be her own grandchildren. A grandmother like that is bound to give a kid nightmares! Only Joash escaped.

Six years later, the righteous priest, uncle Jehoiada, gathered the military leaders, Levites, and heads of family groups to make the seven-year-old Joash king of Judah and to execute Athaliah.

As king, Joash obeyed God as long as Jehoiada lived. He saw to it that the temple was repaired and that the objects for sacrifice and worship were supplied.

But after Jehoiada died, the leaders of Judah came to the king and convinced him to turn away from the temple worship of the true God and to worship idols. God moved Zechariah, the son of Jehoiada, to tell the people that God had turned away from them because they had left God. This so enraged Joash that he ordered the people to stone Zechariah. Later, the king's own servants killed Joash in his bed.

Joash seems to have been mostly moved by others, having no conviction of his own. Not a man to imitate.

PHARAOH: Listening to God

And when the people cried out to Pharaoh for food,
he told them, "Go to Joseph, and do whatever he tells you."
Genesis 41:55 NLT

You're standing in the court of Pharaoh, the powerful ruler of a powerful country. Pharaoh is distressed about a dream that he believes holds great significance. His wise men have been unable to explain its meaning.

A young man is led in. He's a slave, a prisoner, and a foreigner. Surprisingly, the humble young man says that he cannot interpret the dream. But. . . his God will explain its meaning to Pharaoh. He then declares that Egypt will have seven years of abundant harvest followed by seven years of terrible drought.

What does Pharaoh do? Does he accept the word of this man and his God or reject his counsel? Will he ignore the slave from Canaan, or will he take action to save the lives of his subjects as well as people living in surrounding countries? Fortunately, Pharaoh accepts the interpretation as an accurate prophecy of the future. He instructs the young man to guide Egypt through the difficult years.

As you think about the events in Egypt, you realize your life falls in that pattern, too. Some years will be filled with abundance, others with trying times. By accepting God as a guide, you will not only survive but also thrive.

What Did That Man's Name Mean?

Just as today, some biblical names had meanings.
Here are a few of those meanings,
including names of some men in this book.

PAARAI: Yawning

PASEAH: Limping

PAUL: Little

PELEG: Earthquake

PENUEL: Face of God

PETER: A piece of rock

PHILEMON: Friendly

PHILIP: Fond of horses

PHINEHAS: Mouth of a serpent

PILATE: Close pressed

PORCIUS FESTUS: Swinish Festival

PUDENS: Modest

AMOS: Speaking from a Place of Humility

Amos answered Amaziah, "I was neither a prophet nor the son of a prophet, but I was a shepherd, and I also took care of sycamore-fig trees."

Amos 7:14 NIV

If God's Kingdom had a human resources department that carefully went over résumés and contacted every reference, it's not likely that Amos would have gotten far in the hiring process.

Before God called Amos to be a prophet, he made his living as a shepherd and a fruit picker—probably like thousands of other men of Judah at the time. Honorable work, but it didn't provide the kind of professional experience most would think might be needed to preach to an entire nation.

But that's the way God works, doesn't He?

Amos was one of many people God used to speak His truth without what seemed like the right credentials. Think of Moses, a man who wasn't much of a public speaker. And how about Gideon, who was petrified with fear? Then there's the apostle Peter, a common fisherman with uncommon—though often misdirected—passion. And the apostle Paul? Forget it! With his past, he wouldn't even have passed a background check.

Amos was like so many other men God used to speak to the people of his time—unqualified, at least by the world's standards. Yet he preached a message that lives on to this day.

God used—and still uses—people with little in the way of credentials but everything in the way of a calling and a burden for the world around them.

ELIPHAZ THE TEMANITE:
Right—but Wrong

*Then Eliphaz the Temanite replied: "If someone ventures
a word with you, will you be impatient?
But who can keep from speaking?"*

Job 4:1–2 NIV

While Job sits in his misery, the unwitting subject of a challenge between God and the devil, four friends come to comfort him. Their intentions are sincere and they love him, but each tackles the situation from his own perspective.

Eliphaz the Temanite is perhaps the loudest voice in the group. He believes in God, but he has a rationalist approach to how God works. God punishes the wicked, he insists, so it would be in Job's own interest to examine his soul, confess his sin, and be restored.

Like rationalists everywhere, Eliphaz makes a convincing case. But he is hidebound by his own thought process. When Job insists he has done nothing wrong and points out that God doesn't always strike down the wicked, Eliphaz's patience rapidly runs out.

His stance is an attractive one to many. We like to figure things out; we are comforted by cause and effect, reassured by the thought that there is always a rational answer. Job's is the more difficult position to adopt. He just doesn't know. It causes him great distress. But still he trusts.

Eliphaz would have done better not to seek explanations and to have sat with his friend in uncertainty a while— as would the rest of us when we find ourselves judging another's misfortunes.

SOLOMON: A Good Start Gone Bad

At Gibeon the LORD appeared to Solomon during the night in a dream, and God said, "Ask for whatever you want me to give you."
1 Kings 3:5 NIV

King Solomon boldly asked God for wisdom. That gift meant Israel's king made decisions that brought unprecedented peace and prosperity to Israel. That wisdom was sought by dignitaries from throughout the world.

Solomon was used by God to pen Ecclesiastes, Song of Solomon, and most of Proverbs. He judged the people with a wisdom that astounded. It seemed that Solomon understood people, culture, and law, and because he'd requested wisdom, God also gave him health, prosperity, and honor. However, the wisdom Solomon used in leading the people of Israel was not always reflected in his personal life choices.

He married hundreds of wives, and his writings in Ecclesiastes demonstrated a sense of depression and disillusionment. Solomon's wives came from nations God had warned the people of Israel against marrying. In the latter years of Solomon's life, "his wives turned his heart after other gods, and his heart was not fully devoted to the LORD his God" (1 Kings 11:4 NIV). Solomon's actions were evil, and God became angry with him.

A good start never guarantees a great ending. Solomon was one of many biblical characters who started well, but ended badly. Following God is a daily decision that resists complacency while trusting that there is purpose in each step forward.

JAIRUS: Emotional Maelstrom

Then a man named Jairus, a synagogue leader, came and fell
at Jesus' feet, pleading with him to come to his house
because his only daughter, a girl of about twelve, was dying.
Luke 8:41–42 NIV

A parent will do almost anything to prevent a child from dying.

As an official of the synagogue, Jairus undoubtedly knew that the Pharisees were at odds with Jesus. But his daughter's desperate condition drove him to seek the healer. Jairus's act of humility at the feet of Jesus is a sharp contrast to the Pharisees' arrogance in their encounters with Him. And he had some degree of faith that Jesus could help.

On the way to Jairus's house, God gave a further reason for faith when a woman was healed of a longtime affliction. Jesus showed His power in healing the woman, and it was a good thing because mere seconds later Jairus needed stronger faith.

Immediately after, word came that there was no point in taking up the Master's time because the girl had died. Imagine the grief that overwhelmed Jairus. But Jesus told him to stop being afraid, "only believe, and she will be made well."

Despite the ridicule of people at the home, Jesus restored the girl to life.

When we need great faith, we do well to remember the times God has already shown Himself faithful.

PETER: I Won't Do That!

*"No, Lord," Peter declared. "I have never eaten anything
that our Jewish laws have declared impure and unclean."*

Acts 10:14 NLT

Peter, the apostle, was well aware of the moral laws of God
embodied in the Ten Commandments and the ceremonial
laws about dietary restrictions. The dietary and ceremonial
rules made Jews a special people, and to Peter, Jews who
violated them dishonored their national character.

While on the roof to pray, Peter saw a vision of four-
footed beasts, reptiles, and birds let down from heaven. In
a clear violation of Jewish laws, Peter was told to kill and
eat the unclean animals. In one of the most astonishing
sentences found in the New Testament, Peter calls God
"Lord" and tells him "no" in the same two-word sentence.
Two more times the vision repeats with instructions not to
call anything unclean that God had made clean.

The purpose of the vision became clear two days later
when Peter preached to the Gentile centurion Cornelius
who, together with his entire household, received the Holy
Spirit and was baptized. Peter understood then that Gentiles
were to be received into the fellowship of believers without
keeping the Law of Moses.

Peter received both gentle nudging and hard shoving to
point him in the right direction. Like Peter, Christians who
keep an open heart to the Word of God will eventually be
guided to the right choices for their lives.

BARAK: Claiming the Full Blessing

Barak said to her, "If you go with me, I will go; but if you don't go with me, I won't go." "Certainly I will go with you," said Deborah. "But because of the course you are taking, the honor will not be yours, for the LORD will deliver Sisera into the hands of a woman."

Judges 4:8–9 NIV

The Bible depicts Barak, a military leader during the time of the judges in Israel, as a great man of faith—so great that he is mentioned by name in the Faith Hall of Fame in Hebrews 11 (v. 32).

Barak courageously united the warriors from the tribes of Israel and led them to victory over their Canaanite enemies. He also respected the authority of the judge Deborah, setting himself apart as a man who honored the leadership of a woman—something virtually unheard of in those days.

But Barak, as courageous as he was, had a moment of doubt, and it prevented him from receiving the full blessing God had chosen him to receive. Barak had enough faith to take on the task God had set before him—but under one condition, one God never intended. Barak was willing to go to battle, but he placed his faith not in God alone, but also in the leadership of Deborah. For that, he lost some of the blessing God had intended for him.

Doing great things for God requires faith. When we place our faith in God alone, He allows us the full blessing He intends. But we must have the courage to believe Him.

ENOCH: The First Man Not to Die

*And Enoch walked with God after he begat Methuselah three
hundred years, and begat sons and daughters: And all the days
of Enoch were three hundred sixty and five years: And Enoch
walked with God: and he was not; for God took him.*

Genesis 5:22–24 KJV

The generations of Adam in the book of Genesis don't just say how long each descendant lived. It emphatically states that each of them died. Except for Enoch!

After a life that was the shortest in the list, Enoch was taken by God. Everyone else died. Enoch simply vanished off the face of the earth. Why? Frustratingly, the writer doesn't say.

But we are given a hint in the book of Hebrews where it says "before his translation he had this testimony: that he pleased God" (Hebrews 11:5 KJV).

Now, despite the fact that God is everywhere, we're separated from Him by original sin. Jesus died so that gap might be closed—after death. Imagine living a life so pleasing to God that He just can't wait to have you in His company. So He doesn't even wait for you to die.

It's even more impressive when you realize that Enoch lived eight generations after the Fall and only two generations before the Flood. Difficult times to be a man of God.

Plenty of people will tell you that these are difficult and godless days. What better time to follow the example of Enoch, the first man God didn't want to be without?

TERAH: Toward the Land of Promise

Terah took his son Abram, his grandson Lot son of Haran, and his daughter-in-law Sarai, the wife of his son Abram, and together they set out from Ur of the Chaldeans to go to Canaan. But when they came to Harran, they settled there.

Genesis 11:31 NIV

Terah's ancestry can be traced to Shem, Noah's son. His family had settled in Ur of the Chaldeans, but as an older man, Terah gathered those who'd follow and they left town.

Why Terah felt he should leave, and why he didn't complete the trip to Canaan isn't revealed, but we do know that Terah's son Abram (later Abraham) was called by God to be the father of nations. Perhaps God was preparing Terah's son for the final leg of his trip and the challenges he would face. To do that he couldn't stay in Ur. Other passages of scripture make it clear that leaving Ur was important (Genesis 15:7; Nehemiah 9:7).

Because Abram and his brothers were born in Ur, it's possible Terah understood that his son would be better off leaving the cultural influences of the city behind.

Terah was called out of Ur, and he left. His son, daughter-in-law, and grandson (Abram, Sarai, and Lot) followed. Harran became their temporary home until Terah died. Then the three completed a journey to Canaan that would change history.

Are you being led by God into a new venture or phase of life? What definite steps are you taking to make the vision a reality?

JASON: Guilt by Association

*When they did not find them, they dragged Jason
and some other believers before the city officials,
shouting, "These men who have caused trouble
all over the world have now come here."*

Acts 17:6 NIV

News gets around and not everyone likes it.

Paul had been in Thessalonica for three weeks, teaching that it had been necessary for the Messiah to suffer, die, and rise from the dead, and that Jesus was that Messiah. A great many Grecian Jews believed, but some of those who didn't roused a mob to seize and accuse Paul and other believers.

They came to Jason's house, planning to catch Paul and Silas, but didn't find them. Not willing to go away empty-handed, they grabbed Jason and some others and took them to the city leaders. Jason was accused of harboring Paul and Silas and of believing there was another king besides Caesar. The leaders of the mob accused all the believers there of stirring up revolt, though their own rabble-rousing was far more disruptive.

The city leaders seem to have been calm about the whole thing. They took note of who was accused, made Jason post bond, and turned them loose.

We've had it pretty easy, haven't we? Jason was called to account for his faith within days of believing.

PHILIP: Introducing Jesus

So never be ashamed to tell others about our Lord .
2 Timothy 1:8 NLT

Philip was called as an apostle directly by Jesus. "The next day Jesus. . .found Philip and said to him, 'Come follow me'" (John 1:43 NLT). Philip's first action was to find Nathanael (also known as Bartholomew) and introduce him to Jesus.

Like Peter and Andrew, Philip was from Bethsaida, and he probably knew them. Philip is a Greek name, and Philip the apostle most probably spoke Greek. Some Greeks had come to Jerusalem for Passover. They wanted to speak with Jesus and asked Philip to make the introduction. Philip asked Andrew to join him in approaching Jesus with the request.

Most of what we know about Philip comes from the Gospel of John. Not all of the events reveal Philip to have a full grasp of the nature of Jesus. For instance, he was skeptical that the apostles had the means to feed the crowd of five thousand. Yet, he knew Jesus had turned water into wine, and he had seen Jesus do many other miracles.

We don't know how or when Philip died, or what people said of him after his death. What we do know is that he introduced others to Jesus, and that's a fitting way for any Christian to be remembered.

What Did That Man's Name Mean?

Just as today, some biblical names had meanings.
Here are a few of those meanings,
including names of some men in this book.

RAGUEL: Friend of God

RAM: High

REGEM: Stone heap

REHOB: Width

REHUM: Compassionate

REUBEN: See ye a son

REZON: Prince

RIBAI: Contentious

RINNAH: Creaking

ROHGAH: Outcry

ROSH: To shake the head

RUFUS: Red

ANANIAS: Not What He Claimed to Be

*Then Peter said, "Ananias, why have you let Satan fill your heart?
You lied to the Holy Spirit, and you kept some of the money
for yourself. . . . You weren't lying to us but to God!"*

Acts 5:3, 4 NLT

Most of us want people to think well of us. That can be a positive; in fact, the Bible tells us that we should do everything we can to build a good reputation (Proverbs 22:1).

But the desire to be thought well of can also lead us to big downfalls. Ananias, a fallen member of the first-century church in Jerusalem, is a sad example of this truth.

The Jerusalem Christians were selling lands and houses and sharing the proceeds with others. But Ananias and his wife, Sapphira, hatched a plan to sell their property and give only part of the proceeds to the church and keep the rest for themselves.

The scheme came to light when the Holy Spirit alerted the apostle Peter, who confronted Ananias about his lie. Moments later, Ananias lay dead on the ground. Three hours later, his wife met the same fate.

Ananias and Sapphira's sin wasn't a lack of generosity but a lack of honesty. They lied to the church—and to God—about what they had done, no doubt largely because they wanted the Jerusalem Christians to think well of them.

For their sin, they lost everything.

We can fool others, and we can even fool ourselves—at least for a time. But we can never fool God, who knows our hearts and sees our actions for what they truly are.

EPAPHRAS: A Willing Prisoner

Epaphras, who is one of you and a servant of Christ Jesus,
sends greetings. He is always wrestling in prayer for you,
that you may stand firm in all the will of God, mature and fully
assured. I vouch for him that he is working hard for you
and for those at Laodicea and Hierapolis.

Colossians 4:12–13 NIV

We don't know if Epaphras was jailed with Paul, but both men seem to have thought of themselves as prisoners of Christ. What does that mean? Surely Jesus doesn't lock people up!

What He does is show people a love beyond imagining and the incredible wonders of the kingdom of heaven. Both are so far beyond our expectations that anyone beginning to understand them could not force themselves to walk away. Having known Jesus, we become captivated by Him and refuse to leave His work to do our own thing.

Epaphras might literally have been a prisoner for his faith, but he is also a fine example of how our beliefs should never be determined by our circumstances. Being locked up didn't mean he wasn't still working for the kingdom. Paul tells us that Epaphras was constantly in prayer for the new churches, and we know what wonders are often wrought by prayer.

Whatever situation Epaphras was in, he was where he wanted to be—with Jesus! And, in jail or otherwise, he was always doing God's work.

THE THIEF ON THE CROSS:
Paradise Gained

Then he [the thief] said, "Jesus, remember me when you come into your kingdom."

Luke 23:42 NIV

There were three men crucified that Friday afternoon. Golgotha was known as "the place of the skull," and spectators gathered to simply stare or to mock. Jesus had endured the derision and verbal abuse of Jewish leaders, and he faced it once more from a criminal who ridiculed Him from his own cross.

A second thief hung nearby, but recognized Jesus was different. He rebuked the other criminal for the words he'd spoken then said, "This man has done nothing wrong" (Luke 23:41 NIV).

Perhaps a criminal's endorsement meant little to the crowd, but it came from the heart. This thief admitted blame, recognized Jesus' innocence, and asked the Creator of all to "remember" him when He entered His kingdom.

Where one thief expressed sarcasm and ridicule, the other expressed remorse and faith. Hanging from the cross the thief could do nothing to earn God's attention. His past left nothing good for God to consider. He simply trusted in the most profound example of grace. Jesus' words opened eternity to him: "Truly I tell you, today you will be with me in paradise" (Luke 23:43 NIV).

Salvation is easily offered because the price Jesus paid was beyond comprehension. We are left to offer belief or ridicule. One saves—one separates.

JAPHETH: Important Cover-Up

And Shem and Japheth took a garment, and laid it upon both their shoulders, and went backward, and covered the nakedness of their father; and their faces were backward, and they saw not their father's nakedness.

Genesis 9:23 KJV

Japheth, his brothers, and parents had come through the Flood that destroyed all other human life. Sometime later, his father, Noah, planted a vineyard—not just a vine or two, but enough to produce grapes to make wine. Though he had no direct instruction from God about drunkenness, certainly Noah must have seen its results before the Flood. In spite of that, he drank enough of his wine to fall into a stupor in a state of undress.

There are lots of things we aren't told about this, such as: Where was Mrs. Noah, who could have tenderly covered him while murmuring, "You silly old fool," or similar words of comfort. Perhaps Mrs. Noah was busy elsewhere.

Instead, Noah's youngest, Ham, saw him and told his brothers. Again, we aren't told any details of this encounter and have no license to invent possibilities. But Japheth and Shem covered him without looking at him.

When Noah had slept off his intoxication and learned what Ham had done, he spoke a curse on Ham's son Canaan and blessed Japheth and Shem. It seems safe to say that Japheth had no thought of getting a blessing when he covered his father. But God did bless him.

ONESIMUS: Going Home

I appeal to you to show kindness to my child, Onesimus. . . .
Onesimus hasn't been of much use to you in the past,
but now he is very useful to both of us.
Philemon 1:10, 11 NLT

When Onesimus ran away from his owner in Colosse, his flight took him to Rome. In seeking his own security, Onesimus made a remarkable discovery. The man who had converted his master to Christianity, Paul, was in the city, too. But their roles were now reversed. Paul was under house arrest awaiting trial while Onesimus could visit him freely.

Onesimus became a Christian and began doing for Paul many of the same tasks he had done for his owner Philemon. Eventually Paul decided Onesimus and Philemon needed to be reconciled.

Onesimus would return to a city where he had been neither a Christian nor a dependable slave. He must have wondered how the Colossians could be certain of his transformed life. Paul reassured Onesimus in several ways. First, he sent Tychicus to accompany him; he praised Onesimus both in the general letter to the Colossians and in the personal one of Philemon. In addition, Paul wrote one sentence in both letters in his own hand to prove the authenticity of the letters (Colossians 4:18; Philemon 1:19).

Onesimus returned home on faith that he would be accepted as a Christian brother worthy of reconciliation. He understood the importance of making things right.

ASA: The Importance of Finishing Strong

*In the twentieth year of Jeroboam king of Israel, Asa became
king of Judah, and he reigned in Jerusalem forty-one
years. . . . Asa did what was right in the eyes of the Lord.*

1 Kings 15:9-11 NIV

One of the overarching themes in the Bible—especially in
the New Testament—is the importance of finishing strong
in the life of faith.

Asa, the third monarch of the kingdom of Judah, spent
the first thirty-five years of his forty-one-year reign honoring
God in every way he could. He led his nation in instituting
reforms that included restoring the worship of God and root-
ing out idolatry and other sins that had taken hold in Judah.
And after a battle with Egypt in the tenth year of Asa's reign,
Judah enjoyed a quarter-century of peace.

Those things alone could have qualified Asa as one of
the greatest Old Testament monarchs. Sadly, however, Asa
stumbled late in his life, marring an otherwise spectacular
reign. Rather than continuing to trust in the Lord, Asa
sought worldly means to solve his problems—including
forming an alliance with King Ben-Hadad I of Damascus
when the neighboring kingdom of Israel threatened Judah
(2 Chronicles 15:1–16:13).

The Bible commemorates Asa as a good king who did
many great things and who honored God and did what was
right in His eyes. But Asa didn't finish well, and that may
have kept him from being mentioned as one of the Bible's
most important men.

EPHRAIM: First Even Though He Was Second

And he blessed them that day, saying, In thee shall Israel bless, saying, God make thee as Ephraim and as Manasseh: and he set Ephraim before Manasseh.

Genesis 48:20 KJV

We know Ephraim for his childhood and his descendants. Between those two extremes precious little is told of his life, but because he was given precedence over his older brother when both were small and unproven, we can only surmise that God picked him out for a reason.

His father, Joseph, was well situated in Egypt. He made homes there for his brothers and his father. But the "pilgrimage" of Jacob, Joseph's father, was coming to an end. He asked to see his grandsons before he died, so Joseph brought Ephraim and Manasseh to him. The boys were small enough to stand between their father's knees. When Jacob blessed Ephraim before Manasseh, Joseph told him he had made a mistake. The first blessing should go to the older brother, Manasseh. Jacob, who was almost blind but knew what God wanted, told his son there had been no mistake.

So we can assume Ephraim became a worthy man and lived a faithful life. What of his descendants? Well, how about Joshua, son of Nun of the tribe of Ephraim, successor to Moses and possibly Israel's greatest leader in war? It seems God and Jacob knew what they were doing after all when they made Ephraim first even though he was second.

TIMOTHY: All Grown Up

*Timothy was well thought of by the believers in Lystra and
Iconium, so Paul wanted him to join them on their journey.*
Acts 16:2–3 NLT

Timothy started with credentials, became an intern, and ended
up a leader in the church at Ephesus. The apostle Paul trusted
his protégé enough to allow him to instruct the Ephesians on
why some topics should have no place on the church stage or
in Christian life.

The young missionary was instructed to tell the Ephesians "not to teach false doctrines. . .or to devote themselves
to myths and endless genealogies." Why? "Such things pro-
mote controversial speculations rather than advancing God's
work" (1 Timothy 1:3–4 NIV).

With each progressive step Timothy took, Paul passed
on more responsibility and instruction. Timothy became
a master learner. As Paul instructed, Timothy applied the
learning to his teaching.

Paul's final instructions to Timothy were as strong as those
he'd given throughout the young man's training, yet they make
sense for us as well: "Continue in what you have learned and
have become convinced of, because you know those from whom
you learned it, and how from infancy you have known the
Holy Scriptures, which are able to make you wise for salvation
through faith in Christ Jesus. All Scripture is God-breathed
and is useful for teaching, rebuking, correcting and training in
righteousness, so that the servant of God may be thoroughly
equipped for every good work" (2 Timothy 3:14–17 NIV).

Learn. . .apply. . .teach.

JEHOSHAPHAT: Bad Company

*And Jehu the son of Hanani the seer went out to meet him,
and said to king Jehoshaphat, Shouldest thou help the
ungodly, and love them that hate the LORD?
Therefore is wrath upon thee from before the LORD.*

2 Chronicles 19:2 KJV

Sometimes good motives move us to do bad things.

Jehoshaphat was a good king of Judah who strengthened his cities and his army to the point that the surrounding kings feared to attack. He then sent his officers throughout the country with Levites and priests to teach his people the law of the Lord.

God blessed Jehoshaphat's rule with many gifts from his subjects, and even some from the Philistines.

In that atmosphere of calm and plenty, Jehoshaphat made peace with Israel's evil king, Ahab. Maybe Jehoshaphat thought he could be a good influence. After all, the people of Israel were of the same family as Judah.

Planning a joint battle against Ramoth-Gilead, the two kings listened to Ahab's false prophets, who told them to "Go for it!" Wisely and diplomatically, Jehoshaphat asked if there were a prophet of the Lord available. Ahab grudgingly called Micaiah, who said Israel would be without a shepherd after the battle and Judah would go home in defeat.

Jehoshaphat, perhaps feeling too committed to back out with honor, went along to war.

Micaiah had spoken truth. Ahab was killed and the battle was lost. We, like Jehoshaphat, need to know that certain alliances are not God's will.

PHARAOH: A Heart in Denial

Then the LORD said to Moses, "Pharaoh's heart is stubborn,
and he still refuses to let the people go."
Exodus 7:14 NLT

A shepherd from Midian and his brother stood before Pharaoh and demanded the release of the Hebrew slaves. Pharaoh was the strongman leader of the strongest country in the world. He ignored God's command to release 600,000 male slaves and their women and children. Despite the demonstration of God's power—the Nile turned to blood— Pharaoh returned to his palace and put "the whole thing out of his mind" (Exodus 7:23 NLT). His kingdom continued to suffer through plagues of frogs, gnats, flies, and the death of livestock. By the sixth plague, he must have known that resistance was irrational.

Pharaoh denied a power greater than himself. He continued to resist and the depressing pattern continued. More plagues followed: boils, hail, locusts, and darkness. His recalcitrance caused his people to suffer and his nation to be devastated.

The tenth plague caused a temporary change of heart. His own firstborn son died (Exodus 12:29). He released the Hebrews, but then changed his mind and sent his army chasing after them. After pursuing them into the divided sea, the waters rushed over Pharaoh's horses, chariots, and charioteers. The word came back: Pharaoh's army had perished.

Pharaoh has become an example of the serious consequences that come to those who refuse to listen to God.

What Did That Man's Name Mean?

Just as today, some biblical names had meanings.
Here are a few of those meanings,
including names of some men in this book.

SAMSON: Sunlight

SAMUEL: Heard of God

SAUL: Asked

SETH: Substituted

SHEDEUR: Spreader of light

SHELUMIEL: Peace of God

SHIMI: Famous

SIBBECAI: Corpselike

SILAS/SILVANUS: Sylvan, of the woodlands

SIMON/SIMEON: Hearing

SOLOMON: Peaceful

STEPHEN: Wreath

BARNABAS: Encouraging and Strengthening the Weak

Barnabas wanted to take John, also called Mark, with them, but Paul did not think it wise to take him. . . . They had such a sharp disagreement that they parted company. Barnabas took Mark and sailed for Cyprus, but Paul chose Silas and left.

Acts 15:37–40 NIV

It's easy to assume there was perfect harmony among the apostles who took the message of salvation into the world during the New Testament era. But Acts 15 records a disagreement so serious that the teo people parted ways.

Paul and Barnabas traveled and worked together during Paul's first missionary journey (Acts 13–14). The two men were accompanied by John Mark, Barnabas's cousin, but Mark left them and returned home to Jerusalem after a short time.

As Paul and Barnabas planned their second journey, it became apparent that Paul hadn't forgotten Mark's desertion. Paul wanted to leave Mark behind, but Barnabas wanted to give the young man another chance. The two parted ways over the disagreement, and Paul left for his second missionary journey without him.

But Barnabas didn't give up on his cousin. In fact, he spent time mentoring him and encouraging him. In time, Mark became such an effective minister of the Gospel that Paul himself acknowledged that he had become helpful to him in his ministry (2 Timothy 4:11).

In encouraging young John Mark, Barnabas became an amazing example of sacrifice and encouragement to those who are weaker in their faith or have fallen at some point in their walk with Jesus.

EZEKIEL: Taking It Personally

*I looked, and I saw a windstorm coming out of the north—
an immense cloud with flashing lightning and surrounded
by brilliant light. The center of the fire looked like glowing
metal, and in the fire was what looked like four living
creatures. In appearance their form was human,
but each of them had four faces and four wings.*

Ezekiel 1:4–6 NIV

Ezekiel gets straight to the point!

He tells us he is a thirty-year-old exile in Babylon and then—bam! We are hit with some of the most spectacular visions in the Bible: four-winged beings, heads with four different animal faces, fiery wheels, a central figure of molten metal, fire and rainbows, and a throne of lapis lazuli.

God really wanted to get this guy's attention. Even though He had sent His people into exile, He still wanted them to know there was a way back. Prophets like Ezekiel carried the message of redemption to a people who mostly didn't want to hear it.

To hammer home how important this message was, God told Ezekiel he would be held personally responsible for each soul that was lost if he didn't impress on them how they might be saved (Ezekiel 3:17–19).

We might hope that God doesn't hold us responsible for the people we don't share the Gospel with, but Ezekiel's story shows just how important a mission it is and how seriously God takes it.

So, we need to ask, how seriously do we take it?

SIMON THE ZEALOT:
Following with Purpose

When they arrived, they went upstairs to the room where they were staying. Those present were Peter, John, James and Andrew; Philip and Thomas, Bartholomew and Matthew; James son of Alphaeus and Simon the Zealot, and Judas son of James.

Acts 1:13 NIV

Sometimes teachers have to be creative when there's more than one student with the same first name. Multiple students with the first name "Jimmy" might use Jimmy B or Jim-Jim or even Jimmy the Juggler. Jesus chose twelve disciples and three of them shared the same first names, Judas, Simon and James. Nicknames often have meaning. For the latter two disciples there was Simon (also named Peter) and Simon the Zealot.

Some scholars say that his nickname means that Simon had been a member of the radical anti-Roman fighters, the Zealots—but it would have been foolish for him to walk around Roman-ruled Israel identifying himself with such militants.

More likely, "Simon called Zelotes" (Luke 6:15 KJV) simply referred to his zeal. It's easy to think of Simon as one who was passionate about his faith, purposeful in his walk, and trusted with the work God gave him to accomplish.

Would we feel as comfortable being known as zealous, or would we prefer to go unnoticed? Why?

JEHU: In Cold Blood

*So Jehu slew all that remained of the house of Ahab
in Jezreel, and all his great men, and his kinsfolks,
and his priests, until he left him none remaining.*

2 Kings 10:11 KJV

Jehu must have been like a snake coiled to strike, because Elisha told his messenger to anoint him king of Israel, tell him God's command to kill Ahab's family, and then open the door and flee!

It's hard to think about the sort of judgment God ordered.

At once, Jehu took a chariot and sped toward Jezreel. When Israel's king, Jehoram, came out to meet him, Jehu shot an arrow through his chest and ordered his men to shoot Judah's king, Ahaziah, who was visiting Jehoram.

Entering Jezreel, Jehu encountered Ahab's widow, Jezebel, looking from an upper window in fresh lipstick and eyeliner. She told him he'd never get away with killing her son and son-in-law. Jehu yelled to those around Jezebel, "Who is on my side?" Two or three eunuchs looked out and Jehu told them to throw her down, which they did. Her blood splattered the wall and the horses, which walked over her body.

While Jehu ate his supper, dogs ate the body of Jezebel, as God had foretold.

Next, Jehu exchanged letters with the city elders who hosted Ahab's seventy sons, resulting in the heads of those sons being delivered in baskets.

God was satisfied with Jehu's results, but left no comment on his bloodlust.

PHILEMON: The Heart of Christianity

Masters, be just and fair to your slaves.
Remember that you also have a Master—in heaven.
Colossians 4:1 NLT

Philemon lived at Colossi. During one of Paul's visits to that city, Philemon became a Christian and worked with other believers there. Paul continued his missionary activities and later was in Rome under house arrest while awaiting trial. Paul wrote a letter to the Colossians and entrusted its delivery to Tychicus and a companion. Near the end of the letter, Paul wrote, "I am also sending Onesimus, a faithful and beloved brother, one of your own people. He and Tychicus will tell you everything that's happening here" (Colossians 4:9 NLT).

Onesimus? Could this companion of Tychicus be the same slave that had run away some time earlier? Yes, because Onesimus carried a personal letter from Paul written to Philemon. In the letter, Paul warmly praises Philemon for his faith, love for God's people, generosity, and kindness. Then Paul comes to the heart of the matter. In running away from Philemon, the slave had run to Rome, met Paul, and become a Christian. Paul appeals to Philemon to welcome the slave back as a Christian brother: Paul said, "With him comes my own heart" (Philemon 1:12 NLT).

The question of "What did Philemon do?" is unanswered. The letter to Philemon becomes a question for all Christians: What should we do when one who has wronged us comes back seeking forgiveness?

BEZALEL: Equipped by God for God's Calling

"See, the LORD has chosen Bezalel son of Uri, the son of Hur, of the tribe of Judah, and he has filled him with the Spirit of God, with wisdom, with understanding, with knowledge and with all kinds of skills."

Exodus 35:30–31 NIV

When most of us think of God calling someone to do something specific, our minds tend to move toward vocations such as a preacher, a teacher, or a missionary. But an Old Testament character named Bezalel is an example of two important biblical truths:

God needs all sorts of skills to further His kingdom.

He is the source of all the skills and talents that we need to do His work.

Bezalel was a workman God chose for the divinely commissioned job of constructing the tabernacle and its furniture and artwork. He worked very skillfully, creating beautiful structures with metal, wood, and stone.

While we usually think of the skills Bezalel possessed as being the result of years of training and experience—and that was true in his case (v. 10)—the Bible teaches that it was God who then especially anointed him to accomplish the work for which he had been called.

God may not have gifted you to be an artisan, a pastor, or any other worker we usually associate with a "calling." But, through His Spirit, He has given you the very gifts and skills you need to accomplish what He has called you to do for His kingdom.

ESAU: Teaches His Smarter Brother

And the first came out red, all over like an hairy garment;
and they called his name Esau.

Genesis 25:25 KJV

Rebekah didn't just give birth to twins. She was also the mother of two nations who would often be enemies. The firstborn was Esau, who would be a simple but rough man of the hills. His descendants would become the nation of Edom. Holding onto his heel was the second twin, Jacob, the patriarch of Israel.

As they grew up, Esau would have plenty of reasons not to like Jacob. The younger brother sold him food in exchange for his birthright instead of just giving it to him. Then Jacob pretended to be Esau to get his father's blessing.

Jacob went out into the world and made his fortune; then, in a time of need, he turned back for home. He expected his brother to be against him, so he divided his people and flocks (so that some might survive) and prepared peace offerings. Instead, Esau ran up to Jacob declaring that he had his brother back and needed nothing else. But Jacob insisted on sharing the wealth.

A few generations further along, the nation of Edom would refuse passage to the Israelites. The relationship between the two nations would eventually cause God to prophesy Edom a future as an eternal wasteland.

If only the nations of the world could remember what Esau taught Jacob—that despite their disagreements, they were still brothers!

TITUS: Continuing Good Work

But God, who comforts the downcast,
comforted us by the coming of Titus.
2 Corinthians 7:6 NIV

Paul was quick to express gratitude to the missionary partners with whom he served, including Timothy, Silas, John Mark, Barnabas, and Titus, to name a few. Each proved willing to go beyond the milk (easy-to-digest spiritual food) found in God's Word and chew on the meat (spiritual teachings with substance, leading to discipleship).

Titus was commissioned to the isle of Crete to finish the work started by Paul. It's possible he would rather have been elsewhere, but he had a task, and Paul's letter to Titus provided details on how to complete the work.

In this letter we read details of what Titus was to accomplish. The result of his work wasn't to cater to babes in Christ, but to move the Christians of Crete to a deeper walk. In order for Titus to do this, he had to be a mature disciple who'd already moved into a deep relationship with Jesus himself.

Knowing that the work Titus was doing could not be sustained by one person indefinitely, Paul promised to send Artemas or Tychicus to relieve him. Once they arrived in Crete, Titus would join Paul on a trip to Nicopolis.

God has work for us to do also, but it won't always be in the same place or with the same people. Be sensitive to God's leading and change gears when He has new plans for you.

JEPHTHAH: Oops!

*Then it shall be, that whatsoever cometh forth of the doors
of my house to meet me, when I return in peace
from the children of Ammon, shall surely be the
Lord's, and I will offer it up for a burnt offering.*

Judges 11:31 KJV

The men of Gilead had come begging outcast Jephthah to lead them into battle against the advancing Ammonites. As war approaches, Jephthah promises that if God gives him victory, he will sacrifice the first thing that comes from his house to meet him when he returns home. That turns out to be his only child, a daughter.

There has been and continues to be much debate about whether Jephthah actually killed and burned his daughter. Those who believe he did often cite the clear words of an English translation of the account in Judges. The account is less clear in the Hebrew.

Be that as it may, Jephthah was foolish to make a vow with an outcome that was not known to him. First out the door could have been something that didn't even belong to him, a neighbor, or an unclean animal.

Worse, he would have been fulfilling a vow that would affect the life or wellbeing of a person who had not agreed to the vow. The commands of God forbade human sacrifice, so Jephthah would have been wrong to sacrifice anyone. If he was also wrong not to fulfill his vow, at least only he would have suffered any consequences.

PETER: The Sleeping Apostle

In peace I will lie down and sleep, for you alone,
O LORD, will keep me safe.

Psalm 4:8 NLT

Chapter twelve of Acts describes how King Herod arrested Peter and put him in prison to be tried after Passover. Peter could expect no mercy at the hands of this tyrant. The king had put James the apostle to death a short time earlier. Herod's father, Herod Antipas, had beheaded John the Baptist at the start of Jesus' ministry, and his grandfather, Herod the Great, had ordered the execution of innocent children in Bethlehem in an attempt to kill baby Jesus.

Peter's situation would have caused most people troubled sleep, fear, anxiety, or worry. Peter's friends did stay up all night, but they were holding a prayer vigil for his safety.

While his friends prayed, Peter fell deep asleep chained between two guards. An angel came to lead him from prison. A light tap on the shoulder was not enough to rouse the sleeping apostle. The angel had to strike him on the side and tell him, "Quick! Get up!" (Acts 12:7 NLT). The angel then led Peter from the prison to freedom.

Two of the most common commands that Jesus gave Peter and the disciples were "Fear not" and "Be not afraid." Peter had learned that sleep comes easier when a Christian trusts in God to see him through stressful times.

What Did That Man's Name Mean?

Just as today, some biblical names had meanings.
Here are a few of those meanings,
including names of some men in this book.

TABBAOTH: Rings

TABEEL: Pleasing to God

THEOPHILUS: Friend of God

THOMAS: The twin

TIBNI: Strawlike

TIMOTHY/TIMOTHEUS: Dear to God

TOBIAH: Goodness of Jehovah

TOLA: Worm

TYCHICUS: Fortunate

URIAH: Flame of God

UZZA: Strength

UZZIAH: Strength of Jehovah

PHARAOH'S CHIEF BAKER:
Hearing the Truth

When the chief baker saw that Joseph had given a favorable interpretation, he said to Joseph, "I too had a dream: On my head were three baskets of bread. In the top basket were all kinds of baked goods for Pharaoh, but the birds were eating them out of the basket on my head."

Genesis 40:16-17 NIV

It's not easy to communicate bad news, even when we know someone needs to hear it. Pharaoh's chief baker, who was imprisoned with Joseph, must have been thrilled when he heard Joseph interpret the dream of a fellow prisoner, Pharaoh's chief butler, in such a positive way. (You can read the whole story in Genesis 40.) Surely, he must have thought, that means my dream foretells good things for me, too.

However, the news for Pharaoh's chief baker wasn't good. He had offended Pharaoh so deeply that he was about to be executed. And Joseph never hemmed or hawed when he communicated his interpretation of the baker's dream. He simply told him the truth God had communicated to him.

The Bible doesn't tell us how the baker responded to Joseph's interpretation of his dream, only that what Joseph had told him would happen, happened.

It's not easy to talk to the "bakers" in our lives and tell them about eternal punishment for their sins. But just as Joseph told that imprisoned, condemned baker the truth, we as followers of Christ show true compassion when we speak the truth to those we know are lost and dying—then offer them the hope of eternal life.

EUTYCHUS: Dead to the World, But Not to the Word

Seated in a window was a young man named Eutychus, who was sinking into a deep sleep as Paul talked on and on. When he was sound asleep, he fell to the ground from the third story and was picked up dead.

Acts 20:9 NIV

If you have ever felt yourself dozing off during a Sunday service at church, then you might have some sympathy with young Eutychus.

The apostle Paul had arrived in Troas. Eutychus and many others gathered excitedly in a third-floor room to hear what the great man had to say. Paul, of course, had plenty to say and was still speaking at midnight. Eutychus, who had probably been at work all day, dozed off and tumbled off the window ledge he had been sitting on!

Thankfully, someone noticed and raised the alarm. But the fall from the third floor, had a predictable outcome. Eutychus was dead. Paul ran downstairs, threw his arms around him, restored him to life, had a snack. . .and carried on preaching!

If your preacher goes on and on, it might be because he has something to say, something worth going on at length about. Like Paul, he might be speaking words of life. Eutychus got to experience the power of those words firsthand. You and I don't need to fall out a window. We only need to stay awake through the sermon, listen, and believe!

UZZIAH: He Followed God— Until He Didn't

Uzziah sought God during the days of Zechariah, who taught him to fear God. And as long as the king sought guidance from the LORD, God gave him success.

2 Chronicles 26:5 NLT

Judah had a new king. He came to the throne at sixteen years of age, and he had much to learn. While other teenage boys were learning a trade, Uzziah was faced with something a bit more important. He must have been grateful to have such a mentor as Zechariah. During those years when the king honored God and sought His direction, he experienced multiple blessings.

Uzziah upgraded the army's weapons of war and defeated the Philistines in battle. He also fortified the city of Jerusalem.

While northern Israel went through a few kings during Uzziah's reign in Judah, he was able to remain in power, offering safety and security to his people.

However, Uzziah began to believe he was somebody pretty special. He wrongly assumed he could go into the sanctuary of the temple and burn incense. This was not his job, and he hadn't been set apart to manage this sacred duty. The priests reacted to Uzziah with righteous anger. In response to his unrepentant heart, God caused leprosy to break out on the king's forehead. Uzziah would suffer from the disease for the rest of his life.

No matter what God allows us to accomplish, we should never think we are above humbly obeying Him.

JOB: A New Perspective

Behold, I am vile; what shall I answer thee?
I will lay mine hand upon my mouth.

Job 40:4 KJV

Often, Job's story is a pattern for our approach to understanding a great loss. We, too, want to know why bad things happen to good people.

We think of God's promises of blessings and provision of the things we need. We remember His encouragement in Hebrews 13:5 (KJV): "I will never leave thee, nor forsake thee." But some Christians have lost every physical possession and/or their health.

Job searched his memory for any reason that he might deserve what had happened to him. He wished he had died at birth, so he couldn't have lost anything. He listened to his friends tell him he certainly must have deserved what happened, because God is not unjust.

Then Job lamented God's silence about his experience and wished he could plead his case to God. For Job, and us, our concern is always that our distress seems out of proportion to our faults.

Job never got an answer to his bewildered questions. Instead, God asked him a series of questions that showed Job the vast difference between God's power, knowledge, and wisdom and his own. Although he wasn't informed of it at the time, Job himself was being shown as a faithful servant of God. Sometimes, hardships may come to us for no other reason than to demonstrate our faithfulness to those who have not believed, or believers who need encouragement.

PHILIP: Decisive Moments

Brothers, select seven men who are well respected and
are full of the Spirit and wisdom. . . . Everyone liked this idea,
and they chose the following: Stephen (a man full of faith
and the Holy Spirit), Philip, Procorus, Nicanor,
Timon, Parmenas, and Nicolas of Antioch.

Acts 6:3, 5 NLT

Philip (known as Philip the Evangelist to distinguish him from Philip the Apostle) experienced firsthand how the church could grow. When poor foreign Jews in Jerusalem were overlooked in receiving help, Philip was selected (along with six others) to address the concerns of these foreign believers. They successfully did so, and the church remained strong.

Shortly afterward, persecution scattered the believers. Philip traveled into the province of Samaria. The traditional Jews wanted nothing to do with Samaritans. Several centuries earlier, pagans had settled in Samaria; although they worshipped God after a fashion, they were considered heretics. Philip carried the Gospel to members of these hated and despised people, and many Samaritan men and women were baptized. The apostles, then Peter and John, came to Samaria and accepted the Samaritans as fellow Christians.

Philip and the church faced two decisive moments, once in Jerusalem with the foreign believers and again in Samaria. Philip helped take down barriers and increase the number of believers. Just as importantly, he assured people that Jesus loved them even if they were outcasts or came from a foreign country.

THE MAN BORN BLIND:
Taking That One Small Step

*After saying this, he spit on the ground, made some mud with
the saliva, and put it on the man's eyes. "Go," he told him,
"wash in the Pool of Siloam" (this word means "Sent").
So the man went and washed, and came home seeing.*

John 9:6-7 NIV

The account in John chapter 9 of Jesus healing the blind man in Jerusalem raises some questions. Why did Jesus rub mud in the blind man's eyes and then tell him to go wash himself in a nearby pool? Couldn't He have just pronounced him healed and sent him on his way like He had so many others?

It's possible that Jesus healed this man the way He did so that he would have a small part in receiving the healing. He never asked Jesus to heal him, yet Jesus used an unusual—some might even say "gross"—method to heal him. Then He gave him the opportunity to receive that healing by taking one small step of obedience.

Jesus also made it clear to His disciples that this man hadn't been born blind because he or his parents had committed sin, but so that God would be glorified through the work Jesus did in healing him.

This teaches us all kinds of lessons about how God uses people's situations to bring glory to Himself, about how He chooses to do His work, and about spiritual blindness and sight. But it also gives us this important truth, one we may personally experience: when God is in the midst of doing something wonderful—even miraculous— He may ask us to take some small step toward making it happen.

EZRA: The Lawman Comes to Town

*When I heard this, I tore my tunic and cloak, pulled hair from
my head and beard and sat down appalled. Then everyone
who trembled at the words of the God of Israel gathered
around me because of this unfaithfulness of the exiles.
And I sat there appalled until the evening sacrifice.*

Ezra 9:3–4 NIV

Ezra was a real bad-news-bear for the Jews who still lived
in Jerusalem. As an exile he had been far away from the
homeland and the temple ruins—so he now valued them
all the more. As a descendant of Aaron, he was a dedicated
student of the Law.

Many Jews he found in Jerusalem seemed to value
none of these things. Familiarity had bred contempt. They
had diluted their way of life and their faith to a point where
they were hardly recognizable as Jews. By marrying foreign
women (when "Jewishness" is traditionally passed through
the maternal line) they were, in effect, destroying their
heritage. These women also worshipped pagan gods and
would raise their children to do the same. No wonder Ezra
was appalled.

He came among them as a reminder of all they had
given away. . .and no one likes having their shortcomings
proclaimed in the public square. But sometimes it's necessary.

If Jesus came back today, would He think we had
diluted His message? Maybe we need to give that a little
thought before the Lord turns up, like Ezra, pulling His
beard in frustration.

WISE MEN: Honoring the King

*"Where is the newborn king of the Jews? We saw his
star as it rose, and we have come to worship him."*
Matthew 2:2 NLT

Depending on how the original words are translated, Jesus received visitors who could be referred to as wise men, magi, or astrologers. We don't know names, how far they traveled, or how many arrived. We usually think there were three of them because they brought three gifts, but there could have been more.

They dropped by King Herod's place thinking he knew where to find the new king. There were some pretty negative repercussions from their palace visit. Angels told the wise men not to return to talk to Herod, while Mary and Joseph were told to escape to Egypt with Jesus. Soon, an envious Herod ordered all boys under two years old to be killed in hopes of eliminating this rival king.

Mary and Joseph apparently stayed in Bethlehem long after Jesus' birth, and the wise men likely arrived when He was close to two years of age. They left gifts of frankincense, myrrh, and gold. All were symbolic gifts for a king. The family then fled to Egypt and stayed there until the death of Herod. The family ultimately ended up in Nazareth because it wasn't safe for them to return to Bethlehem.

Someday all men will recognize Jesus for who He is. Recognizing Him early is a mark of being a true wise man.

What Did That Man's Name Mean?

Just as today, some biblical names had meanings.
Here are a few of those meanings,
including names of some men in this book.

ZABBAI: Pure

ZABDIEL: Gift of God

ZACCHAEUS: Pure

ZADOK: Just

ZALMUNNA: Shade has been denied

ZEBEDEE: Giving

ZEBULUN: Habitation

ZECHARIAH: God has remembered

ZEDEKIAH: Right of God

ZEEB: Wolf

ZINA: Well fed

ZOPHAI: Honeycomb

JOEL: Warnings and Comfort

The word of the LORD that came to Joel the son of Pethuel.
Joel 1:1 KJV

God has told us nothing about Joel other than his name and his father's name.

Joel's words show that he spoke for God before Judah was carried off to Babylon, and possibly during the thirty years when King Joash was guided by Jehoiada, the priest.

A rift exists between Bible scholars who think Joel described an actual plague of locusts in Judah and those who believe he used locusts as a metaphor for an army that was devouring the crops and destroying property. Either way, Joel calls on the leaders and the people to repent and promises God's grace, mercy, and blessing if they do.

The second half of Joel's message expands on all God will do for the repentant nation, including pouring out His Spirit on all mankind. On the day of Pentecost, it was this part of the prophecy that Peter said was being fulfilled when the apostles spoke in languages they had never learned.

To whom did Joel deliver these words given by God? As with most of the prophetic messages God has preserved for us, there is no mention of an audience. But the people of Judah were expected to hear, and heed. So should we.

Because we can read how God treated Judah according to her actions, we can know what He will think of our behavior.

PILATE: Failure of Nerve

"Take him yourselves and crucify him,"
Pilate said. "I find him not guilty."

John 19:6 NLT

Pontius Pilate, the governor of Judea, would have been much happier at his Roman enclave in the heavily fortified port city of Caesarea. But he was expected to be in Jerusalem during Passover week to maintain order.

He didn't want to deal with this latest problem. Early in the morning, the Jewish authorities had brought an itinerate preacher for trial. They claimed the man called himself King of the Jews and had violated some Roman laws. They demanded He be put to death.

Pilate questioned the prisoner closely and quickly realized the man was not guilty of any crime worthy of death. Pilate told the crowd, "He is innocent." The crowd roared in anger, "Crucify Him!" Pilate saw a riot developing, so he washed his hands of the matter and gave the decision to the crowd—release this "King of the Jews" or a murderer. The crowd chose the murderer.

Pilate, as governor, had the power to convict and the power to set free. He knew the right choice, but instead let the crowd intimidate him into sending Jesus to the cross. Pilate knew the truth but tried to sidestep it. His decision forever linked his name with a failure of leadership.

In every person's life, events occur that require a stand for the truth. How we respond defines how others will remember us.

BOAZ: A Role Model of Kindness and Generosity

*So Boaz said to Ruth, "My daughter, listen to me.
Don't go and glean in another field and don't go away
from here. Stay here with the women who work for me."*

Ruth 2:8 NIV

It would be hard to read the book of Ruth and not see Boaz, one of its key characters, as a role model of kindness and generosity.

Boaz's very first words recorded in the book—a hearty and kindly "The LORD be with you!" to the harvesters working in his field—tell us exactly where Boaz was coming from. And the harvesters' warm return greeting—"The LORD bless you!"—tells us that they believed he genuinely cared about them.

Boaz demonstrated amazing kindness and generosity to Ruth, the woman who would one day become his wife, when he provided for her and protected her as she gleaned leftover grain from his field. It might not seem like showing chivalry to a woman in whom he had a personal interest is all that noteworthy, unless you recognize that Boaz was the kind of man who made godly kindness a way of life.

Every one of us has opportunities in life to engage in acts of kindness and generosity. But when those acts are motivated out of a true love for God and for others, we'll find ourselves doing them for those who have little or nothing to offer us in return.

That was just like Jesus did when He came to earth to save a human race that had built its existence on rejecting God. Yet He showed us compassion anyway.

FELIX: Eternal Life or Gold? Gold!

And after certain days, when Felix came with his wife Drusilla, which was a Jewess, he sent for Paul, and heard him concerning the faith in Christ. And as he reasoned of righteousness, temperance, and judgment to come, Felix trembled, and answered, Go thy way for this time; when I have a convenient season, I will call for thee.

Acts 24:24–25 KJV

Felix had been governor of Judea for years and had become very wealthy from bribes. He wasn't a stupid or uncultured man. He knew about "the Way." He was interested in what these Christians were saying. He may have even been tempted to dabble in it.

So when Paul became his prisoner, Felix kept him longer than necessary. He was hoping Paul would offer to buy his freedom, but he visited often, so he must have also been fascinated by what the apostle had to say. As Paul told him more about Jesus, the governor withdrew, saying he didn't have time for this.

It seems his curiosity had reached the point where he would have to have let Jesus into his life to find out if He was real, but that would have affected his kickbacks. He couldn't let that happen.

Felix was smart. Smart enough to realize that Jesus wasn't a shallow pool to dip your toe into. He's an oncoming wave that will sweep your old life away and leave you with a new, eternal one. And not everyone is prepared to let that happen.

ZACCHAEUS: Small Man in Town

*Jesus said to [Zacchaeus], "Today salvation has come
to this house, because this man, too, is a son of Abraham.
For the Son of Man came to seek and to save the lost."*
Luke 19:9–10 NIV

He was a small man in town with large ambitions. Zacchaeus was the guy who hated crowds because if he wasn't in front, he couldn't see. Besides, he didn't have many friends. It wasn't just his height, but he was a small man at heart. He was a tax collector who sometimes charged more than he was asked to collect. The extra income supported what was likely a lonely lifestyle. When you're known to cheat, people come up with uncomplimentary names.

Zacchaeus heard Jesus had come to Jericho and knew the crowds would be a problem. So he scaled a nearby tree and watched Jesus come closer. Jesus stopped, looked up, and said, "Zacchaeus, come down immediately. I must stay at your house today."

Jesus knew Zacchaeus by name, and He invited Himself to lunch. Zacchaeus was eager to oblige. This encounter with Jesus began an internal change in the small-hearted man. He issued generous tax refunds for his overcharges and discovered that what he most wanted in life was. . .to be found.

Discrimination is not a part of the love language of God. Bring your height, body shape, emotional baggage, and broken dreams. Maybe, like Zacchaeus, you just can't wait to be found.

JOHN THE BAPTIST: God's Messenger

Verily I say unto you, Among them that are born of women there hath not risen a greater than John the Baptist: notwithstanding he that is least in the kingdom of heaven is greater than he.

Matthew 11:11 KJV

The day John was born, his father, Zacharias, foretold that he would prepare the way of the Lord. Zacharias also made clear that the Lord's purpose in coming was to "give knowledge of salvation unto his people by the remission of their sins" (Luke 1:77 KJV).

We're told that John grew strong in the Spirit and spent his time in deserted areas until he started preaching. He knew the scriptures about the Messiah and that he, John, was the one Isaiah spoke of as one crying in the wilderness, "Make straight the way of the Lord."

John set himself to his task with single-minded determination. He spoke to crowds about sin and the need to turn away from it and obey God's commands. He told the people to look at Jesus and to know that Jesus would take away their sin.

John's life was never about himself. He would have neither wife nor family. He would not be rich. He would not have long life. His parents were aged when he was born and probably died before he began preaching. He came into the world for only one purpose—to point the way to the Savior. There is no better purpose.

THE POOR BUT WISE MAN:
Making a Mark

Now there lived in that city a man poor but wise, and he saved the city by his wisdom. But nobody remembered that poor man.

Ecclesiastes 9:15 NIV

The book of Ecclesiastes has many thought-provoking verses: "Is there anything of which one can say, 'Look! This is something new?'" (1:10 NIV); "There is a time for everything, and a season for every activity under the heavens" (3:1 NIV); and "Remember your Creator in the days of your youth" (12:1 NIV); but one of the most remarkable is the story in Ecclesiastes 9:15 about the heroic poor man whose name is no longer known.

Seventy-five years ago the media was slower and the news cycle longer. An unusual event that caught the attention of the public was known as a seven-day wonder. Later, a person caught up in a news event was said to have fifteen minutes of fame. Today, an Internet story can go viral and become an immediate sensation. A person can be thrust from obscurity to overnight celebrity in a few hours.

Yet, fame is fleeting. A little boy lost, an extraordinary rescue, a heroic act—all fade from the public memory with knife-edge swiftness. That's what happened to the poor but wise man. His story is Solomon's way of explaining that activities under the sun (earthly life) can be deceptive and fleeting. The events with eternal importance are those we do for God.

AN UNNAMED BOY: Giving Everything, Even When It's Not Much

Another of his disciples, Andrew, Simon Peter's brother, spoke up, "Here is a boy with five small barley loaves and two small fish, but how far will they go among so many?"
John 6:8–9 NIV

Do you ever wake up in the morning thinking, Today God is going to use me to do something miraculous!

It's hard to imagine the unnamed young boy (mentioned in the story of Jesus feeding more than 5,000 hungry followers) thinking anything beyond his own physical needs as he began his day. He was toting a small sack lunch of two small fish and what in reality was not much more than five small biscuits.

As it was, he was carrying probably barely enough food to nourish a growing boy for the day. But he gave Jesus what he had—and the Lord made it multiply. . .over and over and over, until it became more than enough to feed 5,000 men and who-knows-how-many women and children.

What we have may seem small and insignificant in comparison with what others have to give. But when, in faith, we give God what little we have, He has a way of doing the miraculous with it, of multiplying it far beyond what it once was.

So never think that God can't do a miracle through what you have—even if it's something as "insignificant" as a kind word, a small favor or gift, or a quick reminder that "God loves you, and so do I."

God specializes in using those kinds of things, so be ready to give.

FESTUS: A Governor Governed

*But Festus, willing to do the Jews a pleasure, answered Paul,
and said, Wilt thou go up to Jerusalem, and there be judged
of these things before me? Then said Paul, I stand at Caesar's
judgment seat, where I ought to be judged: to the Jews
have I done no wrong, as thou very well knowest.*

Acts 25:9–10 KJV

Governor Festus must have been confused. He was a man of
authority and power, capable of making things happen as he
wanted. But the matter of his prisoner, Paul the apostle, was
unfolding in a way he couldn't control.

He couldn't understand why the Jews wanted Paul dead,
so he asked him if he would face his accusers in Jerusalem.
Paul claimed his right as a Roman citizen to put his case to
Caesar.

To add to the confusion, Herod Agrippa heard Paul and
told Festus that he might have freed this man if he hadn't
appealed to Caesar. Now, however, Festus was obliged to
send him to Rome.

The matter had been taken completely out of Festus'
hands, and he couldn't understand how it had happened. But
God had already told Paul to testify in Rome—not about
himself, but about Jesus!

Festus had authority and power, but God overruled him.
That's where people of faith have the advantage. When we
feel matters have been taken out of our hands, we can trust
that it's for a very good reason and that a higher "Governor"
is at work!

ZECHARIAH: Minor Prophet, Major Message

At that time the prophets Haggai and Zechariah son of Iddo prophesied to the Jews in Judah and Jerusalem. They prophesied in the name of the God of Israel who was over them.

Ezra 5:1 NLT

Zechariah wasn't the only prophet of his day, but like most prophets he had a message and it affected the entire nation of Israel. Scattered and seemingly weak, the people of Israel had been ruled by others for a very long time. Zechariah had big news—God was going to restore their fortunes, but this wouldn't happen based on the strength of the people. God made it clear He was their strength when He had Zechariah write, "It is not by force nor by strength, but by my Spirit, says the LORD of Heaven's Armies" (Zechariah 4:6 NLT).

Knowing God would bless the people could lead to pride, so there was a need for further instruction, "This is what the LORD of Heaven's Armies says: Judge fairly, and show mercy and kindness to one another. Do not oppress widows, orphans, foreigners, and the poor. And do not scheme against each other" (Zechariah 7:9–10 NLT).

This prophet had a message. He shared that message. That message brought the people together, and this gathering of the people would be needed to introduce Jesus to earth. The world needed this message of love and encouragement shared by a prophet named Zechariah.

JOHN MARK: Strong Finisher

For Demas hath forsaken me, having loved this present world,
and is departed unto Thessalonica. . . . Only Luke is with me.
Take Mark, and bring him with thee: for he is
profitable to me for the ministry.

2 Timothy 4:10–11 KJV

God hasn't told us what Paul's thorn in the flesh was, nor why John Mark left his cousin Barnabas and Paul in the midst of a trip to spread the Gospel of Jesus Christ. In each case, preachers have been eager to form intricate speculations proving the "what" or the "why."

But God's purpose in withholding information in both stories may be that we can better apply the principles to our lives because we don't know the details.

What is recorded about John Mark is that he went home before his job was done, displeasing Paul, and that later on he was trusted to be useful to Paul. In fact, Paul asked to have him sent to him.

John Mark is also the accepted author of the Gospel of Mark.

John Mark's mother was a well-known believer in Jerusalem; a throng of Christians gathered at her home to pray for Peter when he was in jail awaiting execution. No doubt, John Mark also was known, having an audience for his every success or failure.

Many of us have people watching us. Whether we have done well or ill, let's finish well, as John Mark did.

PHILIP: To the Ends of the Earth

*"You will be my witnesses, telling people about me
everywhere–in Jerusalem, throughout Judea,
in Samaria, and to the ends of the earth."*

Acts 1:8 NLT

After Philip's successes in Jerusalem and the well-populated province of Samaria, an angel of the Lord sent him to the lonely Gaza road. Travelers in this isolated region feared robbers and would be reluctant to stop and listen to him.

When he saw a man in a chariot, Philip ran beside it and talked to the man, who was a eunuch serving as the treasurer of the queen of Ethiopia. The eunuch was reading Old Testament scriptures (Isaiah 53:7, 8) that Philip knew referred to Jesus. He asked the man if he understood their meaning and was invited into the chariot. As they rode together, the eunuch became persuaded that he should be a Christian and asked to be baptized.

Ethiopia (Kush, that is) was on the fringes of the Roman Empire—the very edge of the known world. Before he met the Ethiopian, Philip must have wondered what purpose the Holy Spirit had for him in this desolate place. Philip had ministered to Christians in Jerusalem, then he preached to the crowds in Samaria, and now the baptized eunuch would carry the message to "the ends of the earth" (Acts 1:8 NLT).

Christians can be assured that where the Holy Spirit and the Word of God lead them is where they should be.

Scripture Index

Name Index

Go Deeper into the Bible
with These Resources

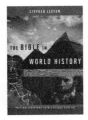

The Bible in World History

What was happening *outside* Bible lands during the time of the patriarchs, Jewish kingdoms, the prophets, Jesus' ministry, and the early church? This fully illustrated reference book breaks biblical and early church history into eight major time periods and shows what was happening in Chinese, Indian, African, and Mayan cultures, among others.
Paperback / 978-1-63409-570-9 / $12.99

The Illustrated Guide to Bible Customs and Curiosities

Why did Bible people wash each other's feet? What was wrong with Leah's "tender eyes"? What did Jesus mean about His "yoke" being "easy"? Readers will find answers to these questions and many more in *The Illustrated Guide to Bible Customs and Curiosities*. More than 750 clear, concise entries are included.
Paperback / 978-1-63058-468-9 / $7.99

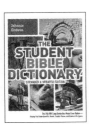

The Student Bible Dictionary

With more than 750,000 copies sold over the past 15 years, The *Student Bible Dictionary* has helped countless readers better understand scripture. Defining and explaining hundreds of Bible words, names, places, and concepts, this book has been expanded and updated with additional information from newer Bible translations.
Paperback / 978-1-63058-140-4 / $9.99